EX LIBRIS

Rachel Sullivan

JESS PHILLIPS
EVERYWOMAN
ONE WOMAN'S TRUTH ABOUT SPEAKING THE TRUTH

HUTCHINSON
LONDON

1 3 5 7 9 10 8 6 4 2

Hutchinson
20 Vauxhall Bridge Road
London SW1V 2SA

Hutchinson is part of the Penguin Random House group of companies
whose addresses can be found at global.penguinrandomhouse.com.

Penguin
Random House
UK

First published in the United Kingdom by Hutchinson in 2017

www.penguin.co.uk

A CIP catalogue record for this book is available from the British Library.

ISBN 9781786330772 (hardback)
ISBN 9781786330789 (trade paperback)

Typeset in 11.75/16.5 pt Caslon 540 by Jouve (UK), Milton Keynes
Printed and bound in Great Britain by Clays Ltd, St Ives plc

Penguin Random House is committed to a sustainable future
for our business, our readers and our planet. This book is made
from Forest Stewardship Council® certified paper.

MIX
Paper from
responsible sources
FSC
www.fsc.org   FSC® C018179

To the women and girls who helped build me
but never got to see the finished result
Mom, Baby Iris and Jo Cox

Everyman (noun): an ordinary or typical human being
'Despite his superstar status, in his movies the actor is able to play the role of an *everyman* quite convincingly.'

Everywoman (noun): an ordinary or typical woman
'Despite her role as a working mother of two, in her job she is able to play the role of *everywoman* quite convincingly.'

CONTENTS

THE TRUTH ABOUT
SPEAKING UP

'You will never be popular.' Not necessarily what you want to hear when you've just started a new job. I'd been in Parliament for just four months when the Rt Hon. Harriet Harman placed her hand on my shoulder and spoke these fateful words to me. I'm not a spiritual person – I don't have faith; I'm your classic smug cynic – but I kid you not, at that moment I felt some sort of baton passing. I'm not messing – I feel a proper div saying this – but I felt something in my heart. I'd stopped smoking around the same time, so perhaps it was coincidentally the moment that my heart started to function properly after twenty-two years of abuse.

Being told that you'll never be popular might seem harsh. Especially when it was said to me by the woman who, aside from my mother, had probably had the greatest effect on my life. This is a woman who fought for women like me to get where I am. She was elected around the same time I was born. Every moment she has spent in our democratic palace has been to make sure that girls like me from outside the Establishment can have a couple of kids, make some monumental mistakes and still stumble upon success and, in my case, one of the most powerful jobs in the land. Don't get me wrong, I deserve a massive wedge of the credit for my own success, but the ladder I climbed wasn't just thrown down to me by Harriet and other women in Parliament; it was whittled by them until their hands bled. Telling me I'd never be popular was her way of saying that it was now my job to build the ladders; that my hands were going to be full of splinters but it would be worth it.

So there I was in the mother of all Parliaments, with the mother of Parliament inspiring me with her knock-'em-dead feminism. She was right, of course. In my sixteen weeks in Westminster I had become, in some quarters, fairly unpopular both in and out of the parliamentary bubble. Quite an achievement when Parliament was shut for recess for nine of those sixteen weeks. In that short time, I'd marked myself out as an angry feminist. A big pink target was scrawled on my back and – whaddya know! – the delegitimisation of my voice had begun. I don't mean to brag, but I count myself in the cool crowd. I was your classic popular kid at school. This new unpopularity was going to be hard to handle.

I might as well get the negatives out of the way now, so we can get back on track. I am writing this as a call to arms to activism after all. They do say forewarned is forearmed, so even though I am tired of saying what I'm about to say, any woman who dares to speak out has to prepare herself for the slow and subtle push for her voice to conform to the norm. These are the top five things people do to infantilise strong (usually female) voices.

Shushing

I accept that this might be going on in the real world – in offices up and down the UK, people might actually be shushing their colleagues – but I can't say it happened where I worked at Women's Aid, so I'm a bit new to it. In Parliament there is a fair amount of shouting, ribbing and sledging. It is often presented as being a very male behaviour, but many of the women on the green benches do it too. Nicky Morgan is a proper mutterer. Anna Soubry jolly well lets you know what she jolly well thinks. I myself am perhaps one of the loudest, but my voice is rarely alone. If I am getting aggravated or am heckling in a debate, I have noticed men from the opposition benches, men who shout and holler all they like, shushing me like I was a five-year-old on a car journey and they were about to miss some vital bit of storyline on *The Archers*. I am *not* a child; do not shush me.

These men have cottoned on to the fact that saying 'calm down, dear' won't play well. So instead they have replaced it with the weaponry of a primary school teacher. On one sublime occasion, a minister on the front bench – a privileged bloke who has never lived on the benefit we were debating – wanted silence for his oh-so-uninformed view on what gets mothers back to work. He looked at me like I was a pramface commoner, fag in hand, screaming kids round my ankles, and shushed me. 'You're not my dad,' I responded. 'Don't you dare shush me while the men shouting around me get no such treatment!' There it is: paternalistic shushing, as if the women in the Commons are nothing more than infant children, there to present an acceptable image. I say to you, good sir, you can take your shushing shushes and stick them up your shushing arse!

If anyone ever shushes you, my advice is to call it out. Ask the man in question, 'Did you just shush me like a child?' They will then be forced to verbalise their dislike of your opposition to their views and will fall apart almost instantly.

'You would say that'

This is an absolute killer. If you care about something or have been identified as a person with a certain position (i.e. feminism), immediately your insights are no longer legitimate. No one says to their GP, 'You say I've got tennis elbow, do you? Well, you would bloody say that.' My advice is to simply reply, 'Yes, I would say that because I am both learned and experienced in this field, so what I say is based on evidence. What about you?'

The fear of a pigeonhole

If only I had a pound for every time someone had said to me, 'Be careful you don't get pigeonholed with the whole feminism thing.' As if the fact that I fight for women not to be murdered and raped means that I don't also have opinions on road safety, the economy and foreign policy. My pretty little head can only deal with one thing at a time, you see. No one ever said to Andy Burnham, 'Watch out, dude, your ten-year campaign for Hillsborough victims means everyone is going to think you only care about football crowds.' No, in that time he managed to be a treasury minister and Secretary of State for Health, and also hold a variety of shadow ninja positions. No one ever said to George Osborne, 'Mate, always chatting about the economy will make people feel like you are a one-trick pony.'

Women with a cause suffer from these accusations simply because they are women. If their cause is women too, they must be reminded of how narrow this is all the time, for fear that something might actually change. I say ignore these comments and care about what you care about. Faking it, like so many things in life, is a pointless exercise that will ultimately leave you dissatisfied.

'You are an attention-seeker always chasing publicity'

Oh what a classic way to shut me up! To make me feel guilty for getting publicity for the things I care about. When I stood up in the Commons on International Women's Day and read out the names of 120 women murdered by men in a single year, every newspaper wrote about it. I made it into the *New York Times*. For a moment I imagined Carrie Bradshaw and her friends discussing it in their fancy clothes in some trendy Greenwich Village brunch hangout. Should I be feeling guilty that people were talking about something that needs talking about? Jeremy Corbyn is in the papers every day, but I doubt he gets called a publicity-seeker. When he was a backbencher, as I am, and was famously marched off by the police in front of the hacks' cameras at an anti-apartheid rally, I doubt anyone said, 'God, he likes himself, he's only doing it to get a spot on *Russia Today*.' On the contrary, he is a man of principle, whereas I – a woman – am considered to be like someone on *The Only Way Is Essex*.

The whole point of being a campaigner is to get publicity to change things. It's the sodding job. I have long campaigned for sustainable funding for refuges in the UK because they are forced to survive year to year on uncertain budgets. It took a campaign by the *Sun* in partnership with Women's Aid to make the government pay attention. Publicity matters. When people call me an attention-seeker, they do it to silence me, and I'm ashamed to say it works. I will withdraw from interviews and avoid noteworthy campaigns for a few months after I've been splashed across the public consciousness. I'll bet you anything you like no man with a cause ever did the same.

But I say to you now: don't do it. Don't listen. Line up every possible platform you have: TV, newspaper, magazine, podcast, radio. Tell the world what you care about, because it makes them care too, and we need people like you to speak up.

They threaten you

The previous four things are often subconscious acts carried out as a result of our continued existence within a patriarchal society. They are not exclusively done by men. We are all guilty of unconscious bias and its associated behaviour. But this final act is committed by true baddies. If they cannot silence you by undermining you, if they fail to make you feel so anxious about your actions that you can't sleep, then the threats roll in. Every day I receive threats. They range from death and rape to warnings of unemployment. Plots to deselect me and others like me from our seats in the House of Commons are the most common.

But this isn't specific to me, or to other MPs. This happens across the land. In every town someone is being called in to their boss's office and being threatened; more subtly than Internet bullying, but threatened all the same. We all have to rub along together, so we should bend and mould to our environment. I get that. Threats are different; threats come about because of a perceived imbalance in the established power structure. They are designed to squash. My best advice is to call it out if you can. I can't imagine anyone in Westminster would threaten me, because I would sing like a bird and everyone would want to listen (one of the reasons why they don't want you to have publicity).

If any one of these five devices is ever used to shut you up, you are winning. It turns out that not being popular actually means not being popular with the kind of people you wouldn't want to go on a date with or find yourself in the caravan next door to on holiday. Next time someone says, 'I know this really matters to you, I'm just worried it might mean people don't take you seriously,' what you should hear is 'Goddammit, people are taking you seriously!' Never in any rom-com or coming-of-age-drama did the popular kid emerge smelling of roses. Nobody cheers when the person who always does well does a bit better. If people come after you for being a success then shout it out, shame them to their faces and amongst their peers; it's what they're trying to do to you. Let's all relish our unpopularity. Let's take back the tag and wear it as a shield. Let's say sod the idea of toeing the line. Let's be unpopular together, because I sure as hell don't want to be unpopular on my own! That would be no fun at all.

THE TRUTH ABOUT
GROWING UP

On an otherwise unremarkable day in 2013, Twitter exploded with the hashtag #tweetyour16yearoldself. The normally acidic social platform turned instead to the kind of inspirational quotes people normally reserve for crap memes written in Comic Sans atop stock images of footprints on the beach: 'It gets better, you can do it', 'You can do anything, be anyone', 'Listen to your parents; turns out they were right', 'You know how everyone thought you'd amount to nothing? Keep going, they were wrong.' It was one long lament about how crappy it is to be a teenager and how being an adult is way better. This is not my experience, so I wrote, 'You are nowhere near as good as you think you are. Take yourself down a peg or two.'

More recently, in 2016, Sajid Javid, the then George Osborne apparatchik Tory Business Secretary, wrote a public note to his sixteen-year-old self: 'Work hard, never stop learning and stay true to yourself and your family.'

I imagine this is exactly what his sixteen-year-old self actually did and he was rather too unimaginative – or too chicken – to tell himself anything different. Personally I would tell Sajid's sixteen-year-old self, 'Loosen up, dude. When you are older, your every waking minute will be watched by journalists, so do all the wild things you want to do now while no one is watching. PS In 2016, when you go on a junket to Australia while the British steel industry crumbles, you will look a douche. Perhaps rethink that one.' But hey, his version made for a good bit of Conservative ideological pull-yourself-up-by-your-bootstraps soundbitery and, let's face it, was probably written by a 22-year-old political advisor named Ben from Tunbridge Wells.

When I was sixteen, I needed to be taken down a peg or twenty. I was not a quiet young woman; I was in-your-face and bold as brass. I was a teenager in the era of girl power, Brit Pop girl bands and grunge. I remember deciding that Courtney Love would play me in a film of my life, which might give you an idea of my place on the shrinking-violet chart. No one could tell me what was what because I knew better. The reality is of course that, like most teenagers, there were endless times when I didn't tell the truth or speak up when bad things happened. Being a teenage girl is to live your life in a decade of contradictions, utterly vulnerable but completely averse to the idea of being vulnerable.

Before I worked with abused young people and before I had my own children, I thought my teenage years were pretty happy. In my school canteen they used to sell those long ice lollies that we call tip tops in Birmingham (I believe others call them ice pops). In the summer all the girls would buy a couple and go and laze around on the grass outside, whiling away our lunch hour tattooing the names of the boys we fancied into our legs with a compass. Oh, the glory days of being fourteen. One day I went to buy my quota of cola and blue raspberry tip tops only to be told that they had been banned in school because they were unladylike. What kind of ridiculous fool looks at a bunch of kids eating frozen E-numbers and thinks, 'By golly, those girls look like they are performing fellatio on those long bright blue shards of ice. This must be stopped immediately'?

There were some wild times, though – too wild for a kid of fourteen. I look back in horror at some of the stuff I thought was normal and acceptable. I can see now the many times I should have spoken up, been the bold, brave girl I thought I was. The things I bragged about while smoking fags around the back of the gym should have been shared with the police instead.

We had endless lessons at school about not bowing to peer pressure. It was presented to us like some faceless demon, an actual thing that could hurt us, and something that we should avoid. It was always suggested that bad people caused peer pressure and weak people succumbed to it. The reality of the slow drip-drip-drip of wanting not to stand out that comes with being an adolescent, and how that grooms young people to take risks, was never put across well. Not only did I bow to peer pressure, I almost certainly generated it. We all did. Despite how oh-so-original we all thought we were, the reality was about constant subtle assimilation to be like everyone else. Looking back, the absolute coolest kids, the ones everyone actually liked, were the ones who didn't just join in with the crowd. My mate Hannah, who was a super brain, who never smoked or drank, who went to youth theatre, got good grades and was kind to people, ended up being the most popular girl in school. She was so comfortable in her own skin, so funny, authentic and sweet, that everyone in every clique liked her. She became head girl when the students were balloted because she was admired by all. I think if there was a league table of who has been a bridesmaid the most times for fellow pupils, Hannah still easily tops it.

Many years on from my school days, I find myself standing in front of a classroom full of thirteen-year-olds, about to dig deep and talk to them about sex. Not the comfy kind of respectful sex you have when you are in your thirties and have been married for ten years. To be honest, I think I would find this more cringeworthy: nobody, but nobody, wants to hear about mom* and dad

---

* Every time I write about being a mother, I receive comments about my use of the term 'mom'. Just so you know, it's not only the Americans who use it; in Birmingham and the wider West Midlands we say 'mom' too.

sex. No, I am there to talk to these young people about rape and sexual exploitation. I'm here to lecture them, but with fun, run-around-the-classroom training riffs.

When I was thirteen, I would have looked at the rather dumpy woman at the front of my classroom and thought, 'Whatever, love' – or whatever it was we said in the early nineties. I'd have probably sucked my teeth as if I were some sort of rude girl, not the girl from a nice-ish bit of Birmingham I actually was. I thought I was all that and then some. I thought I could handle myself, that I was untouchable. When I was thirteen, I thought I was the feminist I am today. I wasn't.

Like many girls, I professed feminism while pretty much capitulating to everything that since then I have trained girls not to do. My gang of mates thrived on being the coolest. Being the coolest meant having boyfriends way older than us. Oh, how very sophisticated we thought we were when our male friends would pick us up from school in their cars. Nothing says cool like a bunch of girls in uniform driving past their bookish peers in a parade of Vauxhall Astras or Novas. We thought we were having fun, and most of the time we were, but bad things used to happen too. I remember one of my mates having to kick her way out of the back of a clapped-out van some bloke had taken her into so he could have his way with her. Attempted rape, you say; a macabre anecdote to be feasted on for weeks was what we saw. We didn't tell our parents and we certainly didn't tell the police. Instead we mulled over every detail, sucking it dry of every last drop of drama we could get. I remember being in the local pub when I was about seventeen and my mate's boyfriend – who was ten years her senior – appeared to have sold her to another man in return for a bag of weed. We joked and laughed about how we would have a whip-round to buy her back. Today I call this sexual exploitation; back then I swooned over the idea that these edgy men found us so desirable.

They weren't edgy; they were criminals. If memory serves me right, I heard years later that one of them was in prison serving quite a hefty sentence for a violent rape. It hurts me deeply to say this, but I'm sure if we had known this at the time, we wouldn't have thought it anything but glamorous.

The feminist I am today wants to scream at young women not to fall for it. The feminist I am today wants to yell from the rooftops at all the men who thought having a teenage girl as an accessory was acceptable. I want to go into every classroom in the country and say to all the young people obsessing over who has lost their virginity or not that in no way does having sex with a random person at a party or in the back of a car make you cool; it makes you pretty much the same as every other kid I knew when I was growing up. If anything, it is dull. What makes you cool is being yourself; being fearlessly who I am is the beginning, middle and end of why I have been a success in almost all areas of my life. Have sex when you want to, not because Becky came back from Marbella and said she had had sex with a lad from Newport, because at the end of the day, Becky is probably lying.

After dragging myself through my A levels, I went off up north to Leeds University, where I read economics, social policy and history. I had started out studying politics and history, but it might be a surprise to hear that I found politics a massive disappointment. I had thought the faculty would be full of radical socialists, fevered with activism. I had images of discussing feminist theory in incense-scented rooms with batik wall hangings. Instead I found loads of posh kids from the south – mainly Tories – discussing the philosophies of old white men. In my second year I changed to social policy and economics because it was about stuff that actually affects people now. I have never been one who wanted to theorise all day; I like action rather than words. I focused my studies on welfare benefits and the welfare state, and, in history, on women's work.

I was not at all studious at university. I rarely attended lectures and went to the bare minimum of seminars. I got the reading lists in the first week and just did it by myself, with some help from my mom, who was a history scholar herself. More to the point, she was the woman paying the newly introduced fees, and she was determined to get her money's worth. When you dedicate your life to bettering yourself through education as my mom had done, and then spend a good chunk of your life campaigning for education and opportunity for all, it is a slap in the face when you find yourself paying for an education for your lazy daughter who is determined to learn little more than how to be amazing at *Countdown* and the art of making roll-ups with one hand. My mother dragged me through my degree, demanding I send her every essay I was meant to be writing. To say that my efforts were a disappointment to her would be an understatement, although she rarely let on what a massive pain in the bum I was.

At university, I was not part of any societies; I did not join in with anything. Nowadays I spend my life with people who were deeply steeped in one political student movement or another. They seem to be part of a network I just don't understand. To me, my NUS card was good only for getting 10 per cent off at Topshop. I went to university in 2000, when politics was on a sort of even keel. My main memories of university are of laughing with the houseful of girls I lived with, and watching endless box sets of *Friends*.

I managed to work my timetable so I was only on campus on Tuesdays and spent most of my time back home in Birmingham. The truth about this period of my life is that I had stopped speaking up for things. Blair was in power, the things that could only get better were getting better and the Labour Party activism I had been so steeped in through the eighties and nineties seemed not to reach me any more. I didn't want to get involved with stuff or be brilliant. I just wanted to get through it.

I think perhaps I never really wanted to go to university,

but it was expected of me at the time. I had always got good grades at school even if I had been a pain. Everyone was going; it was just what we did. I never felt that I needed liberating by leaving home; my life had always been pretty liberal. I didn't know what I wanted to be and I still marvel at the idea that we expect seventeen-year-olds to make a decision that categorises them for the rest of their lives. I don't regret it now I have the piece of paper, but I did not have a great thirst for learning that needed quenching, so going to university felt functional rather than desirable.

This was the time when I was supposed to be growing into an opinionated, learned adult deciding what my future was going to be. In fact, I was going backwards. Turns out life isn't like magazine articles or rom coms. Mostly, I wanted to disappear, which I set about doing by starving myself for months on end. There was a six-week period when I ate nothing but popcorn, until I weighed a little under nine stone, which when you are five foot eight and have HH boobs means you look totally emaciated. Like so many girls, my weight was a way of keeping control of things – it was more about my head than my waist.

Between the ages of eighteen and twenty-one, it is safe to say that men controlled my outlook on life. While at university, I had the clichéd boyfriend-back-at-home whom I missed. I would have thrown it all away to stay with him. My mom had married my dad at eighteen and they were still madly in love forty years on, so I never bought the pervading argument at the time that settling down with your first proper boyfriend was probably not going to be the best option. He wasn't even a very good boyfriend; he was a drunk who smoked too much weed, had little ambition and used to cheat on me all the time. I remember catching him snogging a girl in a photo on the website for Snobs nightclub in Birmingham.

To be fair to my first love, he had not been dealt the best hand. He was a young carer for his mom, who had MS, and his male role models, namely his father, had not been good. I'm afraid I was the terrible cliché of a young woman who thought she could look after everyone. The trials of becoming a proper grown-up while still essentially being a child were tough on me. I seemed to cast myself in the role of woman-as-carer very early on and failed to see the toll it was taking. I thought he needed me to be around to keep him well and happy, and even though outwardly I still appeared self-assured, in my head I placed all my worth in the care of the men in my life. When it wasn't my boyfriend, it was my brother.

As a child, I had been the bolshie (as in both Bolshevik and confident) girl, the tough cookie who could and would stand up to anything and anyone. My youngest brother Luke had quite a different role to play. The age difference between my siblings meant that we split neatly into two groups; my parents called us the 'Bigs' and the 'Littles'. Sam and Joe – the Bigs – were both born in the early seventies, whereas Luke and I were born just twenty months apart in the early eighties. The two of us were close, very close. We spent our childhood together while our brothers were off being all teenage. Later, we hung out together, copping off with each other's friends, partying together and coming down together. Even though he was older than me, I was in charge. It turns out that if your parents constantly drum into you that boys are no better than you, that you can do anything they can do, it sinks in. Maybe it sank in with Luke too, but with different consequences.

Luke had always been a troublesome teenager. He was soft and gentle; too soft and gentle. We always thought he was special because he was born on 29 February so only had a birthday every four years. We celebrated every year but he got special treatment on his real birthday. At sixteen, we would joke, he was only four. I'm sure the two things are unrelated, but we certainly infantilised him his whole life, and in many ways we still do. He had always had someone around to boss him about, so when he went off to secondary school without me or any of his comfortable bossy friends, he did not find it easy. He went to three different secondary schools, being either kicked out or absconding for so long they took him off the register. Luke was the person who bought me my first packet of fags when I was eleven, telling me that Lucky Strikes were made out of desiccated coconut and that menthol cigarettes cured colds and were good for your chest. Instead of shielding me from risk, like a big brother in our patriarchal society is meant to, he took me along for the ride so that he could convince himself it was not that bad. Like all people with bad habits, pulling others in with him was part of his strategy to convince himself that nothing was wrong.

In the time I was away at university, Luke's problems became fairly dark and twisty. The year after I left home, although it was probably far sooner if he was honest, he became a heroin addict. For the first year or so, my parents didn't know; all they knew was that he smoked weed and occasionally nicked their belongings. For a long while when I was at university, I was coming home to try to look after him. We only ever confided in Joe, our older brother, mainly when Luke had got into some sort of trouble I couldn't get him out of. I tried to pay his debts, keep his secrets. I just tried to be with him as much as I could, as if somehow watching him all the time would magically make it better.

Anyone who has ever lived with a drug addict will know that they are impossible to look after. Fights are the most common outcome of any attempt to care. The addict will put you at risk without even a thought, lying to you constantly. I wonder if, when they tell you they need money for bus fare or new shoes for a job interview, they actually believe it is true themselves. Last time I got on a bus it didn't cost a tenner, but a small bag of heroin costs exactly that.

I wanted so desperately to be the person who helped Luke. When you believe you can stand up to anything, that bravery and courage will solve all your problems, it is heart-crushing when no matter what you do, nothing gets better. There is no doubt that my experiences with my brother were my education: they gave me the best training and ultimately the drive to have a career working with vulnerable people. It is no surprise that every day of my working life since has been spent trying to improve the lot of people whom society fails to understand and protect. To so many people, junkies, rebellious teens, battered wives, refugees, or people with severe and enduring mental health problems and trauma are 'other'. My experiences with Luke showed me that they were 'us'. I spent my childhood and early adulthood speaking up for my brother, trying to be his voice; it made me realise that people who don't have a bolshie sister or a close family might need a voice too. Every time I stand up in the House of Commons, I try to speak for people who are forgotten; I try to adjust attitudes and end prejudices. I think every family has a Luke, every family has something dark and sad; if more people spoke up about it, perhaps we could make all the families who are struggling feel like their efforts were less futile.

Luke is thirty-seven now. I am wary of saying too much, but at the time of me writing this, he is well. He is clean from the drugs and is being a good enough partner, a pretty good dad, an awesome uncle, an okay brother and an average son. I will reserve judgement about how far he has come. I have spent much of my life feeling hope, pride and disappointment like a revolving door. I've learnt to take each day at a time and just be glad when I don't end up in A&E or searching my house to see what he has nicked when he pops over.

My childhood and coming of age was a rich tapestry full of brave characters not afraid to make their voices heard. There were times when I followed the crowd, allowed myself to become someone else's idea of who I should be. People write to me and say they wish they could be more like me, that I am so brave, so willing to say 'sod it' to the world, but I wasn't always like that. I've followed the crowd, I've let men tell me what to do and think. I'd like to do something sterner than tweet my sixteen-year-old self; she needs a proper talking-to. As they get older, women often cast themselves in roles they think are expected of them and push aside their own sense of self, put themselves last in the queue. When I was trying to look after Luke, I should also have tried to look after myself a bit better, seen myself as a patient instead of always the nurse. When my first boyfriend didn't want to change anything about his life, I should have been less willing just to throw my lot in with his. If I hadn't been worrying about him, spending all my time and money keeping our relationship together, I might have used my time at university to do something worthwhile, join in, discover stuff. Even the bravest, most self-assured little girls in society all too easily become stereotypical nursemaids. I'm not saying we shouldn't take on caring roles in our families, I'm not saying we shouldn't bend and be flexible. I am saying that we should never let young girls' voices be stifled because the cool kids take the mick, and that women shouldn't automatically be the ones who step up and do all the caring.

I have various tattoos that were once upon a time decorations to celebrate parts of my beautiful body. There's a small Chinese symbol (I know, it was the mid-nineties) on my belly that I had done when I was fifteen. Then, it was about an inch from my belly button; today it's drifted a long way left, about six inches from where it started its clichéd life. I also have what is affectionately called a 'tramp stamp' of lotus flowers at the very bottom of my back. I've no idea where that has ended up as I can't see it, and for this I am grateful.

I once had a perfect midriff, and these markings were designed to draw the eye to my assets. Make no mistake, this is exactly what I thought my midriff was: an asset. I think people assume that a self-assured feminist like me has always been a bastion of high-kicking body confidence. In fact I was the same as every woman or girl, putting my worth into the way I looked. When my body was the conventional sort of perfect – big boobs, tiny waist, hourglass perfection – I was confident about it, but not for my own sake: I was entirely dedicated to the idea of male gaze. I even had a scratch-and-sniff belly top, with strawberries emblazoned across my bust. For me, the days of girl power were anything but. I knew as a teenager and a young woman that I had something to be envied by women and desired by men. Even better, I thought, when men much older than I was seemed to marvel at my physique. I never appreciated how healthy I was, how I could run a hundred metres in just under fourteen seconds or swim for miles and miles without stopping. These days I climb a flight of stairs in Westminster and need a sit-down. My health was never at the forefront of my mind.

Recently I was sitting on my usual Wednesday-night train from London back home to Birmingham. Seated opposite me were two women of African origin in Islamic dress. I assumed they were Somali, although I have no evidence for this other than the fact that, having lived all my life in one of the UK's most diverse cities, I can recognise certain physical aspects as well as cultural trinkets that point to a person's origin. They were quiet and snoozing. Sensible women.

Across the aisle from us sat about ten young people emblazoned with the livery of the phone shop EE. They were all in their late teens or early twenties, all from London, and were travelling, I think, to some EE training event in the Midlands. They were not quiet or snoozing. They initially caught my attention because, while they were loud, I struggled to decipher what they were saying, mainly because I could only understand one word in five. There was a lot of 'fam' and 'bare' being thrown around. In Parliament, in comparison, I am undoubtedly in the younger, more connected group of people. This is no benchmark; it's not difficult to be relatively in tune with the zeitgeist when the average age of your colleagues is fifty.

In the four seats directly parallel to me sat two of the

young men and two of the young women. The women were asking the men to tell them what their first impressions of them had been. These unexceptional-looking, inarticulate men didn't hesitate, and started giving the young women in front of them scores out of ten in a series of categories, with some added analysis to boot: 'You've got really good hair, and when you turned round I thought, yeah, that's a good face, so I'll give you a seven out of ten for your face.' To the second woman: 'It's hard to say, I can't remember when I first saw you, but I think I'd rate you a bit less than my girl here.' To which the young woman responded, 'Fair enough.' The women were not horrified by this conversation; they were encouraging it, but in no way reciprocating the assessments. Mine would have been: 'You've got the smug face of a young man who holds the power in this conversation, but in fact you are skinny and frankly generic-looking.' I had become completely transfixed with the conversation as it continued and was making no bones about staring agog.

The second, quieter young man had clearly noticed that one of the women was consistently scoring higher than the other; in a moment of what I think he believed was chivalry, he offered to the runner-up, 'I think you've got really nice hygiene.' This could have been urban-speak for something really complimentary, for all I knew, but it sounded a lot like 'You're not as pretty but you are clean.' The young woman looked delighted. By this point I had a very visible scowl on my face, stunned by the degrading claptrap in front of me. I was about to interject, but before I could open my mouth, the now wide-awake Somali woman in front of me beat me to it. 'Hygiene, hygiene, HYGIENE! Don't talk to women this way.' I would have added more, but her elderly maternal indignation seemed a fitting verdict on their woeful standards. The youngsters quietened down and sat in shamed silence, and as seats became free at Milton Keynes, the whole group shuffled further down the carriage. I sat giggling with my new-found friend, picking over the bones of what we had heard all the way to Birmingham New Street, and concluding that in that one conversation of four bold-as-brass, confident young people, feminism had died.

In their report *The State of Girls' Rights in the UK*, launched in 2016, Plan International cites research from the All-Party Parliamentary Group on Body Image and the Ofsted and Dove survey on girls' attitudes that shows:

- Between one third and half of young girls fear becoming fat and engage in dieting or binge eating
- One in four seven-year-old girls has tried to lose weight (seven-year-olds!)
- Over a third of girls feel they should try to look more like the pictures of girls and women they see in the media
- 12 per cent of girls say they would consider cosmetic surgery

- 70 per cent of teenage girls don't participate in certain activities because of body-image anxiety
- two in five 11-to-21-year-old girls have desisted from participating in 'fun activities' because they were anxious about their appearance
- 30 per cent took part less in class or at work because of body-image issues.

When I look at young women, they all seem so beautiful to me. Real, boundless beauty, full of life and possibility. I wish they could see that rather than aspiring to be like women in magazines. I am not claiming to be any kind of cover girl, but I have been on the cover of a magazine. I have undergone many photo shoots, for Sunday supplements and broadsheet centre pages. I can tell you now, there is nothing natural about how those pictures are taken. What appears like one photo in print in reality takes hours and hours to produce. Hair and make-up women wait just out of shot, fiddling with your fringe, constantly faffing with your lipstick. You are made to stand in the weirdest, most unnatural positions to make you look good. At one shoot, apparently I wasn't wearing the right colour for the look, so one of the journalists suggested we swap outfits. This woman was about a size 10, and one of my boobs would not have fitted in her entire top. It was a kind if not barmy suggestion. When I am on telly, I spend ages in make-up (make-up women always have the best gossip). I went to see my husband's Auntie Liz recently, and at the sight of me in the flesh, she said, 'Oh you do still look like one of us. On the telly you look like a different woman.' So anyone aspiring to look like a person in a magazine is also aspiring to sit around in a cold room all day, in front of a window with just the right light, arms bent back in a weird way, with a person constantly slapping stuff on your face and pulling your hair. I'm all right, thanks.

The idea that women are withdrawing from activity because of the way they look is absolutely heartbreaking. Anyone who has ever done this, I urge you to think about the men and boys you know. Are they knockouts? The world is full of men who are funny-looking, or at the very least not picture-perfect, getting on with doing fun stuff. Breakfast television is full of men who wouldn't get a modelling contract sat chatting away next to absolutely drop-dead-gorgeous women. It is maddening that women feel they have to be both clever and amazingly beautiful to step up and have a go at things.

My hairdresser informed me while foofing up my barnet that you can get a boob job on the never-never. I remember, as a teen, mindlessly thumbing through the Grattan and Littlewoods catalogues and marvelling that you could buy a pair of Reebok Classics for only 59p per week for four years. Young women today can get boobs and pay later. The mind boggles at what happens if you default on your payments. I once worked with a woman who had been raped; after her rapist had been convicted, she received a sum of money from the Criminal Injuries Compensation Scheme. When I asked what she was going to spend it on, she told me she wanted a boob job. At first

I thought it was sad that this woman still saw her value as a sexualised object, but I was wrong: she felt she was taking control of her body. I'm not snippy about cosmetic surgery, I think a woman's body is hers to do with as she pleases, but I do worry about young girls thinking that getting a boob job on the cheap is a good idea and will somehow turn them into strong, confident women.

I wish I could say from the dizzy heights of the career ladder that the way women look doesn't matter. I wish I could say that women feeling anxious and judged by their appearance is a teenage phenomenon. It isn't. Alison McGovern, the Member of Parliament for Wirral South, is one of the most beautiful women I know, inside and out. She is a strong, confident woman and when she rises to her feet to speak in the House, she stands tall. She is constantly encouraging women in the Commons to play in football teams or take part in charity tugs of war; she wants us to use our bodies to show our strength. She has the most gorgeous, thick, treacly auburn hair and in my head she is Adrian Mole's true love: the goddess Pandora Braithwaite. She has an Amazonian presence created by her confidence, stature, wit and intelligence. I look up to her both literally and metaphorically.

During one of our many chats on the phone when we try to keep each other going, Alison commented that she had convinced herself that she didn't have the right sort of body to be on TV. My response was simply, 'Bab, if you don't, then we are all screwed.' I wonder if Boris Johnson ever gets on the blower to David Cameron and says, 'I really don't think the camera is kind to me.' Alison knew perfectly well how ridiculous she was for feeling this way, but still she felt it. She was famously castigated for showing a bit too much cleavage on the Channel 4 news while talking economics. Not by anyone with any sense; just some sexist fool who said that her 'prominent cleavage' distracted her male observers from hearing what she was saying.

Women like me and Alison fight back from sexist crap like this. We call it out, shine a light on the dumb stuff people say to us. We do all we can to show that women can be anything they want to be. The crap we get about our bodies, about the way we look, must be publicly ridiculed. The truth is, though, that when you are trained throughout girlhood to believe that the way you look matters, as adults it is impossible, even for amazing, powerful women, to stop that stuff sinking in.

When Theresa May wakes up in the morning on the cotton-sheeted bed in 10 Downing Street, the first thing she has to think about is not Russia bombing Aleppo or the fact that the UK currency is spiralling out of control thanks to Brexit; no, she thinks, what am I going to wear in order to face these challenges and avoid comments about my appearance? When Tony Blair woke up in the same bed (I'm certain the sheets have been changed), he had no such concerns. 'Boring suit again today, Mr Blair?' I sometimes wish women had a uniform as men do, although I do get to wear Converse in the House, something few men would try with a suit.

Every day of our lives women are told we have to look a certain way, our bodies need to be a certain size and shape, and yet if we live up to those standards we have become a massive distraction for the men around us. Theresa May should be able to wear frumpy clothes – a tracksuit if she wants – as long as she can rock up and be decisive, controlled and intelligent. I am not as thin as I'd like; I will forever aspire to be the young woman who was a size 10 with lickable tattoos on her beautiful flesh. Yet that woman was unhappy; she felt out of control, used, manipulated and desperate to be loved. The woman I am today is a woman I am proud of. I'd want to be her friend; I'd definitely want to go out dancing with her. This version of me has an amazing husband, brilliant friends, smashing kids and a good job. This woman has lived an incredible life that has provided hundreds of cracking anecdotes that make her a laugh at a dinner party. If only this woman could be pleased with the size of her bum.

Technology has come a long way in my lifetime, but sadly not so far that you can actually tweet your sixteen-year-old self with helpful advice. So many young people come to me seeking some magic formula for becoming a politician, or a successful and happily married mother. They expect me to be able to say, if you study for this degree, get that work experience, marry in your twenties and have your children young, then Bob's your uncle, you will be a success. If they were to follow my lead, they would have to be a bolshie six-year-old, a smart-arse, risk-taking, fag-smoking teen and a very unproductive and overburdened undergraduate. Failing the twin blessings of inbuilt privilege and wealth, which definitely helps, there is no formula. The only advice I can give to help you grow into a successful adult is just try to be your best, honest self.

THE TRUTH ABOUT
STARTING A NEW CAREER

When we start a new job, or dare to think we should, most people's instant reaction is self-doubt.

I've read a lot about the idea of impostor syndrome. I am certain it is not a purely female phenomenon. I know for a fact that men suffer from it too, but I do think it runs deeper in marginalised groups such as women, black and ethnic minorities, disabled people and those from less well-off backgrounds. I know that I would feel a complete spare part if I turned up to be an engineering apprentice; similarly, my husband, who is a qualified lift engineer, would feel like an impostor in a very real and crushing way if he was called to attend the meetings I go to. So I don't think it is only us females who feel unworthy in our places of work. I have, however, witnessed some really brazen examples of men who definitely didn't feel it when they really should have.

One of the often-reported manifestations of impostor syndrome is the different ways in which men and women react when applying for a new job. The commonly held view is that a woman will not apply for a job unless she meets at least 90 per cent of the required skills, whereas a man will apply even if he only ticks half of the boxes. When I worked at Women's Aid, I was one of the lucky people who got to sift through hundreds of applications when we were recruiting new staff. In every single job advert we ever publicised, and in every recruitment pack we wrote, we included the statement: 'This post is advertised under s7 (2) D Sex Discrimination Act; due to contact with service users this post is advertised to female applicants only.' The statement was not hidden, it was not subtle; it was front and centre in every advert. There were many criteria laid out in the individual job specifications. There was certainly wiggle room on every aspect and we wanted to give opportunities to people starting out if they could show us they had something to offer. We really only had one hard-and-fast line that could not be crossed: you had to be a woman. Without fail, at least two men would apply for each of these jobs. They would look at the advert and think, yeah, that sounds like me, completely failing to recognise the very explicit failing in their candidacy. This is obviously anecdotal, but I think it well reflects the truth in the idea that certain men have a self-assurance problem.

I'm sure many people reading this will think me hypocritical. I'm famed for my confidence; hell, I'm so confident I have spent my evenings writing this book about how very confident and self-assured I am and how you should be too. I'll let you in on a secret. I am terrified most of the time. Every single day I have to force myself out of the door, into a meeting or up onto my feet to make a speech. In my job I get invited along to lots of events. Every day in Parliament I attend a reception for some charity or good cause. In my constituency I am asked to give out awards at schools, to cut ribbons on new playgrounds or new businesses. I am not at the required level yet to have a bag carrier, someone who goes around with me and organises my travel. I can't imagine I ever will be, so I usually go by myself to these shindigs. En route, I always have to give myself a talking-to, I have to fight the constant urge to turn around and go back to the comfort zone of my office.

Recently I was invited to some big fancy industrial strategy launch in Birmingham. I turned up to a huge warehouse on an anonymous industrial estate, dutifully got my badge from the registration desk and entered a room full of men in suits talking industry and golf. I didn't know a single person in the room, so I did what most people do in those circumstances: I pretended to be on my phone and went to the loo for an extended amount of time. For the first few minutes of every event I feel nervous; 'spare' is probably the best way to describe it. I often convince myself that my invitation was a mistake. I don't know if it's a good thing or not, but the way I cope with this nervousness is by being really bold, by becoming an overexaggerated version of myself. When I feel really uncomfortable, I don't shrink, I grow. People are far less sympathetic to this coping strategy; a woman who sits quietly when she is anxious is far more tolerable to most audiences.

Everyone has had that awkward first day where you don't really want to sit and read all the policies and procedures but you have to pretend to so you don't look like a third wheel; you try to look useful while basically being useless. I remember on one occasion when I was working behind a bar, I decided to take all the glasses off the shelves and clean underneath them in order to appear busy. Within minutes, the after-work drinking rush had poured in, none of the glasses was in the right place and the seasoned bar staff were rolling their eyes at me, the keen but useless team member who had made their jobs harder. As a waitress I spent hours and hours polishing cutlery to try and look occupied before I realised everyone else just went out the back for a smoke in the quiet periods or danced around the kitchen to techno. Everyone else seems to know what they are doing, and jargon is thrown around, always a sign of exclusivity. The House of Commons is exclusivity on speed. The entire place is designed to scream in your face, 'You don't belong here.'

When you are elected to Parliament, the returning officer hands you an envelope. When your victory is announced, it's usually 6 a.m. and you've been awake for at least twenty-four hours. It is not the best moment, perhaps, to give you the instructions for your new job. I left my envelope in my car, thinking there was nothing in it, that it was a simple formality. I only looked inside it on the Saturday morning when I got into the car to go and do the shopping; it said 'See you in Westminster on Monday.'

When I was elected in 2015, I hadn't expected (a) to win, or (b) to start for at least a week. All the pre-election polling had pointed to a hung parliament. Never trust the polls. (Note to self: don't say that sentence out loud. I have in the past, and to an untrained ear it sounds as if you belong in UKIP.) I had been informed by a baroness in the know, who had spoken to Black Rod (weirdest, most medieval sentence ever; if this doesn't make you feel like an impostor, nothing will), that Parliament would not be in session for at least a week after the election while the powers-that-be brokered a deal about who would be our supreme leader. Turns out one should never trust Black Rod – no wonder we slam the door in his face every year. The Tories had won a majority and in fact I was expected in Parliament less than seventy-two hours after winning my seat.

In my envelope was the telephone number for the Houses of Parliament travel office, who were tasked with sorting out travel and accommodation for MPs from outside London. I called them and asked for prices for hotel rooms for three days for myself, my husband and my children. It is not every job that will allow you to take your kids along on your first day, but I wanted them to understand why our life was going to change. I wanted them to be part of it with me; after all, they were making sacrifices too. Asking to bring my children appeared to be like asking if I could bring a nuclear missile with me. After endless back-and-forth conversations, I was quoted a price of over £500 per night. Where I live, that is a month's rent. In the end, we packed up our sleeping bags, drove to London in our camper van and slept on the floor of a friend's flat in Brixton. On my first day in my fancy new job, I had had about two hours' sleep, thanks to a six-year-old kicking me in the face all night. As I walked through the doors of the Palace of Westminster, my children by my side, I felt quite sure that the slick suited and booted men around me had had more than twenty minutes to get ready for their day. I'll wager that Ben Howlett, Stephen Kinnock and Alex Chalk, all of whom were elected on the same day as me, hadn't had to negotiate lost shoes and an argument about who was going to sit in the front of the van before taking their seat in Parliament.

I did – and still do – feel like an outsider in Parliament. This is not an uncommon feeling. In the early days of being in Parliament, new MPs are not yet allocated offices. This means you arrive at work and have nowhere to go. When asked by Martha Kearney on BBC Radio 4 in my first few weeks how hard my new job was, I said so far it seemed to be just drinking coffee and having chats. I had no idea that there was a post room filling up with mail for me; by the time I went to pick it up, there was an actual sack full of it. I had nowhere to take this sack, so I sat on a bench in one of the lobbies and started to go through it. I looked like Phillip Schofield receiving the competition entries on *Going Live*, but with no helpful gopher. I had no computer, and to be honest, I don't think I knew what I would be using it for even if I had one. Like every Member of Parliament before me, I had to make up what my job was. What I wanted it to be. This is exactly the same as every job I've ever had. Fake it until you make it.

I suppose it could be said that I have a pretty successful career. Much of it has been down to luck, right place, right time and all that jazz. There is, however, one thing I think I have done well, something that I would encourage anyone who is starting out to do. Say yes to things. If Sophie who works in my office is reading this, I can tell you now that she is screaming at the top of her voice that this is terrible advice. Every single day she tells me that I should say no to more things than I say yes to. She is in charge of managing my diary and is fiercely protective of my time. I frequently go rogue and agree to things without telling her until the last minute, making me an absolute pain in the bum to work for. So Sophie, I am eternally sorry; however, I stand by the fact that I am a yes person. In every job I have had, I have put my hand up to volunteer for the thing that scares me. I don't allow myself time to sit back and assess if it is a good idea or not; I just give things a go.

I remember as a young teen sitting around watching boys play computer games, endlessly practise tricks on their skateboards or master the art of DJing. So many teenage girls do this; they are bystanders to their own lives. I pretended to like things just because the boys I fancied liked them too. I would painfully and awkwardly pause tapes – and latterly CDs – and transcribe the lyrics to gangsta rap (meaning that I can now face down most Dr Dre-based lyrical exchanges; this is a skill that comes up more than you might think). I pretended not to like the stuff I actually liked and watched loads of really boring films about the Vietnam War. No, I do not love the smell of napalm in the morning. When I was about seventeen, I met Alex, who was a revelation. She hung round with boys she fancied, just as everyone did, but if someone was having a go at DJing, she made sure she was up next (warning: she really overuses sound effects and plays the Birmingham Crew repeatedly). Not a kickabout or computer-game tournament would go ahead without her wading in and demanding a turn. The most glorious thing about her was that she did not give even one toss that she might make a complete plank of herself. To this day, at times when I might need some motivation, she will send me an amazing video of herself falling flat on her arse while dancing in a pub garden. She is by far the coolest person I know. Even though she goes scarlet with embarrassment when she does commit a gaffe, she always throws herself back into any game or task as if she is in the final of the 100 metre sprint at the Olympics. She is a professional have-a-goer. She says yes.

There is a stark difference between saying yes to doing

things and presenteeism. Presenteeism is management-speak for the opposite of absenteeism. It basically involves being at your desk from 7 a.m. to 9 p.m. every day. It is often practised by the person who comes in and then moans all day about being ill. It is also favoured by hot shots who want to suck up to their boss. Frankly, if you can't do your job in the allotted hours, either you or your boss has got a problem. Anyone who has ever worked part time – which most women with children will have done – knows that even if you are only paid for four days, you are most likely doing the exact same job you did when they paid you for five. Don't say yes to ridiculously long hours for long hours' sake, but do say yes to being the person who gives the presentation at the annual meeting. When an opportunity comes up to have a go at something, some training or scheme, say yes. Don't be that person in the meeting who says, 'This is never going to work.' Nobody likes that person. Give up on whataboutery and give things a go. Do do things you weren't asked to do if you think they are a good idea. It is always easier to apologise for initiative than it is to seek approval.

I started at Women's Aid as a sort of PA, but I saw that funding was the main issue affecting the organisation so I redrafted myself in that role. I researched loads of different funders and sent my boss details of how each one presented an opportunity. I used Google to research and then email businesses or government departments asking them if they were interested in what we were doing, and would tell my boss about the ones that came good. When my boss was double-booked or one of the managers couldn't make an event, I put my hand up to deliver the training, or go to a strategy meeting to take notes. I always felt nervous. Even now, when I am drafting an email to ask for something, or to put myself out there, my finger hovers over the send button; I am scared about whether I might look like a presumptuous fool, or too big for my boots. I spend a lot of time thinking, sod it, and I run my mother's mantra through my mind: 'Nobody lost an eye, so it can't be that bad.' (This little internal monologue did not help me on the day I took my son to have surgery on his eyes for a bilateral squint, but at almost every other time in my life it has worked.)

Since becoming a politician, I seem to do a hundred terrifying things a day. When *Question Time* called and asked me to go on the programme when I had only been an MP for six months, I did the ridiculous thing of saying yes. Don't think I wasn't crapping myself for weeks beforehand. I was. In the week prior to going on, I didn't sleep at all, and spent every spare moment reading newspaper after newspaper. I researched stuff that would never come up in minute detail. Want to know about the Brexit effect on the car industry? I'm your woman. Ask me about immigration shifts in Lincolnshire (where the programme was filmed) and I can quote the stats at you. Turns out I ended up talking about how I had been to a McDonald's drive-thru in my dressing gown, which strangely enough I had not prepped for.

When the *Spectator Life* editor got in touch with me and asked me if I would appear on their magazine cover with an interview with Julie Burchill, I said yes. Only afterwards did I bother to read her back catalogue of, shall we say, robust character assassinations of politicians and then think for a second: perhaps agreeing to be interviewed in a Tory publication by a woman not known for holding back on the criticism wasn't the best idea. Fortunately we got on like a house on fire. Don't get me wrong, I don't say yes to everything. I was recently asked to go on a reality TV show about herding sheep in Bavaria. I won't make a fool of myself in lederhosen, but I will take a risk to put myself forward when I feel scared.

The reason you are reading this book is most likely because you have heard of me. The reason you have heard of me is because I make a lot of noise. Shameless self-promotion is what many people call it. What I say to these hecklers is, if you sit around waiting for other people to promote you, it's no wonder I have never heard of you. If a woman pushes herself forward, she is accused of embarrassing self-aggrandising. If a man does it, he's considered a go-getter. Why are we women so embarrassed about being ambitious? In all my jobs I have tried to make myself indispensable to my bosses. I wanted them to think they couldn't lose me. That doesn't happen by accident; it happens because you promote the work you have done. There is, of course, a fine line between blowing your own trumpet and pushing yourself forward.

Usually recognition for your work is measured in pay and/or responsibility. I have had to dig deep and ask for both. It was excruciating to do so, but I survived. I am sure everybody finds it excruciating – we are British, after all – but while men might find the asking difficult, women struggle more because bigging yourself up is less natural to most of us. I reminded my boss of all the extra stuff I had done in my job; I reminded her of the times I'd made her life easier and had to listen as she reminded me of some of the times I'd made it harder.

The first thing women have to do is recognise all the stuff that they are doing for free. If I look back at my career and the career of my husband, who incidentally was always paid more than I was until I entered Parliament, there is a stark difference in the value we placed on our time and effort. My husband is incredibly hard-working, but he would not have worked a minute past 5 p.m. without being paid overtime. He would often work back-to-back shifts through the night, but for every hour he clocked up, he had a call-out charge and a standby fee. I, on the other hand, would sit up till the small hours at home, working on this document or that policy. I would spend my weekends sewing curtains for a refuge or picking up new kitchen equipment for hostel flats. I would gladly take a call at 10 p.m. from a distressed colleague whose computer had crashed, meaning she had lost all her training documents for her 9 a.m. seminar, and offer to knock her up some more. I was never paid a single penny for these thousands of extra hours, nor did I expect to be.

My husband used to call me a mug, and he probably had a point. We women should not so easily fall into the routine of being wives and mothers at work. We must recognise the value of all this stuff we do for free. Every shift we cover, everyone's ass we save in a crisis, should be pointed out to our superiors when restructuring, appraisals and pay rises come around. My husband never for a second allowed the long hours he worked to be diminished: had they not paid him extra when his colleague called in sick, or there was a tricky job that would run all night, he would simply have put his tools down and gone home. I did the extra work not out of the goodness of my heart alone, but because I wanted to be recognised as an asset. And I didn't do it without reward: I was promoted three times in two years.

For some reason when we talk about why women don't rise up the ranks, we seem to want to make ourselves responsible for the fact that society is sexist. I really dislike the discourse that blames the gender pay gap on the fact that women don't ask for pay rises or that we are too meek to be promoted. The University of Wisconsin in the US and the University of Warwick and Cass Business School in the UK undertook a study of 800 employers in Australia (where records are kept on pay requests) and found no difference in the likelihood of asking between the two genders. Australia still has a 17 per cent gender pay gap. The truth is that our bosses are often men; when they are considering who to promote, they think of themselves in that situation and so already the image of a striver in their mind looks like them.

I recognise that bigging yourself up is not always easy, but I think a good strategy for pushing yourself forward at work is to find an ally to do it for you. I suppose the whole union movement is based on this principle. Where I worked there was a woman called Amy who became my ally. She had a completely different job from me, so my elevation would never have threatened her or been at her cost. She would gently nudge on my behalf, remark on how well I'd done at things, pass comment on how much extra I had taken on. Similarly, when I saw that a member of the support staff was going the extra mile, offering to help with some of the development stuff that really wasn't their responsibility, I would make sure that I mentioned it to our boss.

I suppose I am saying all this because I think people put me and others like me on some sort of pedestal. I was given an award once at Clarence House by the Duchess of Cornwall for helping to raise the spirits of my community after a series of nasty arson attacks on our street. She thanked me for my remarkable work and congratulated me on being an exceptional individual. I told her that I believed that down every street in the UK was someone just like me who could roll up their sleeves and help their neighbours. I am not exceptional at all; I'm just really good at promoting what I do. People think I am cut from some sort of elusive cloth, and that as a woman with a fearless voice I am different. Every brilliant and fearless woman I have ever met has been utterly terrified most days. No one is perfect; some people are just better at appearing so than others. There is nothing I have done in my life that most other people couldn't have done. In the words of Public Enemy (those teenage years were not wasted), don't believe the hype, things are far less complicated than they seem. People who succeed seem to want to make it look as if it was really difficult, that they had some sort of magic formula, but if that's true, I have no idea what mine was.

I'm not belittling the hard work I put into things. I am dangerously addicted to work. I definitely overburden myself and take on too much pretty much every day of my life. However, I do have a cunning way of dealing with this as well: what I like to call the 'that'll do' approach. I am not a master craftsman; I do not have a job where a detailed amount of precision is required. Every teacher who sent home a report about me described me as 'slapdash'. When I used to write huge contract tenders or funding bids as a charity fund-raiser, I would attend training sessions by fancy consultants about 'writing the best bid' or 'how to develop your organisation'. My colleague Kat and I would read books and pamphlets on the subject and joke that we were going to write a similar guide, called, *That Will Do, Just Send the Thing*.

So many of us pore over things for hours, scrutinising each and every word until there is no life left in the idea and anyone who might have been interested has given up and gone home. Part of the condition of impostor syndrome is having no confidence in what you have done and always wanting it to be just that bit better. I have pretty much lived my life trying to make things good enough, rather than perfect. Every time I rise to my feet to speak in the House of Commons I have usually written my speech just minutes before the start of the debate, or sometimes even during it. On many occasions I have simply spoken from my gut. I always mess something up, stumble on something. Nine times out of ten I lose my thread a bit and have to try to get back on track. It has never been perfect, but it tends to be effective.

On the day when I read out the names of the 120 women murdered by men in a year, I had written my speech at 5 a.m. on the morning of the debate. With only hours to spare, I set about researching every single woman on the list to find out where she lived and who her MP was so I could send each individual an article about the death of their constituent. I made some mistakes in this process, sending things to the wrong MP, and ultimately I ran out of time and had to ask for help. Afterwards, a few MPs approached me and asked whether I had spoken to the families to check it was OK. I hadn't. I wasn't saying anything that wasn't already in the public domain; I was just collating it. In any case, it would have been an impossible task. How would I ever have found them all? Many of the women had been murdered by their husbands or had left no families.

Had I overthought this task, I would never have made that speech. A speech that was written about in hundreds of newspapers all over the world. Domestic violence making the headlines. Thousands of people, including many of the families of those murdered, have written to me about how powerful it was. I think it was the first time a woman had received a round of applause in the House of Commons. To give a voice to those women was – and I imagine always will be – my proudest moment. If I had worried about the logistics of doing it weeks beforehand, wrung my hands about making sure everything was perfect, it would never have happened. I have found that almost without exception, the things I have done that people have praised as exceptional or brilliant were done in haste.

I have never had a life plan. I do not set myself targets for my career. I could never give anything other than a complete bullshit answer to the question 'Where do you want to be in five years?' Five years before becoming an MP, I didn't plan my route to power. Someone suggested it to me and gave me a nudge, and I thought, sod it, I'll give this a go. I have met many men and some women who absolutely did have a plan and worked the numbers. In politics, especially when considering political leadership, there are a lot of planners. Parliament is full of people biding their time, negotiating favours, working and waiting for their moment to shine. I imagine that pretty much without exception, every man in the House of Commons has at one time or another sat back and thought, I could be the boss of this show. The women, it seems, are just happy to be there at all.

I am certain that to get women to say sod it and give something a go, they need cheerleaders along the way. We have to be those cheerleaders. If we see a woman with potential, we should tell her and then pester her with opportunities. I think businesses call this shoring up the pipeline. Women are less likely to see themselves in management roles or as leaders, because let's face it, we've all grown up seeing the world led by men. I wish it wasn't the case, but I know from my own experience that I had to be asked to step up. My slapdash and reckless nature definitely helped me not to overthink myself into a state of disbelieving fear, but I still needed that push. So now I am a pusher. We women will only succeed if we all start pushing each other.

Whenever I speak up, it's usually fairly widely publicised. I've become known for showing my emotions a bit, spilling my feelings. In a debate about VAT on tampons, I spoke about having my period and needing to wipe down the seats of Westminster. I sat and cried great childlike sobs of grief in the chamber of the House of Commons in a debate about the rise of racial hatred following the EU referendum vote. I wept for my murdered friend Jo Cox, who wanted the world to be a better place; I felt we had failed. Most weeks I scream, shout, cry or throw up. I give up, get back up, fight and make up. This is not unusual; I'm a fairly dramatic sort. There is no job I have had where I haven't drafted a self-indulgent resignation letter that was never sent. I think every day that I am doing a bad job, regardless of the evidence to the contrary. I doubt myself just like everyone reading this doubts themselves. No matter how much others criticise my work, no matter how hurtful my colleagues, my bosses or my opponents have been, no one ever comes close to being as mean to me as I am to myself. I suppose what I'm saying is, cut yourself some slack and give everything a try once. Well, maybe not sheep-herding in lederhosen.

THE TRUTH ABOUT

EQUALITY

I'm going to ask you now to put down this book, close your eyes and think for a second about a mayor, a leader, the person in city hall fighting your corner. Don't think of an actual individual whose name you know; just imagine a meeting room where someone is in charge and they are commanding a business leader to invest in their town, their city, their region. No matter what you do to fight my obvious point, the person you are seeing in your head is a man. I bet he is also white.

In 2016, every single one of the Labour candidates selected to run in the regional mayoral elections was a man. Steve Rotheram in Liverpool and Andy Burnham in Greater Manchester both hail from northern towns, and Rotheram was also a bricklayer. They are the image of what the Labour Party is striving for: the common man elevated to power to represent the 99 per cent. Bristol has a black mayor; in London, the Labour Party selected and elected a Muslim mayor, no mean feat in a time of intense Islamophobia. All these men act as symbols of a century of class struggle: the son of a bus driver getting a top job demonstrates that the founding fathers of the Labour Party have done their job and done it well. The 99 per cent have beaten the elite, yet the 51 per cent (women) are nowhere to be seen. The 51 per cent within the 99 per cent should act grateful somehow that their class has won. 'Stand up for your rights' is replaced with 'stand by your man', who really *does* give a toss about your rights.

Recently we've seen the widespread apathy about politics challenged. Across Europe, big populist political movements have sprung up. People have occupied. People have taken to the streets, painting banners and banging drums. People have worn Guy Fawkes masks manufactured in sweat shops to fight capitalism, and used their New Labour 'education, education, education' to draw up witty banners and build effigies of Tony Blair to burn. In the UK, politicians have indulged the demands of many for their voices to be heard, with the result that we are now leaving the European Union. We live in a time when views have become so polarised, so embittered, that a man walked up to a political representative and shot her down in the street.

Online petitions, growing protest movements, social media and instant access to politicians has brought greater engagement of people with politics. The rise of politicians such as Jeremy Corbyn, Nigel Farage and Boris Johnson in the UK, and Bernie Sanders and

Donald Trump in America, speaks to a changing political landscape and the search for personality politics. People crave humanity in their representatives, rather than spoon-fed lines from a zeitgeist adviser. We seek someone who is just like us, an 'everyman' – someone who really is *representative* – to replace the idea of an establishment of people who are all the same. However, the irony in every example of these 'just like me' politicians is that they are exactly that: men. Rich white men from privileged backgrounds. I'm so disappointed that the thing people find great hope in as something different looks to me to be exactly the bloody same as what went before.

Parliament is meant to be the democratic equivalent of our world: it is our society in miniature. I've been walking around it for over a year now, and I can't say it looks anything like the society I come from. I could best liken it to a cruise ship: it has bars and restaurants, a gym, a hairdresser and the level of diversity I'd expect to see on a *Spirit of the Seas* voyage around the Azores. It is not just the building itself; it is the entire area that is eerily beige. When my husband came down with me when I was elected – only the third time he had ever been to London in his life – he commented with genuine concern, 'Where are all the old ladies around here?' In the entire time we were in the area surrounding the Palace of Westminster, he had not seen one old woman pulling her trolley to the bus stop; he had not seen a single parent with a buggy or gang of teenagers smoking fags and acting out. All he had seen were people aged between twenty-one and fifty – and most of them were men. 'I'm a bit worried about you being here too long,' he said. 'It seems to me they have culled all the old ladies.'

When you enter Westminster after working at Women's Aid, it is a sharp shock how few women roam the halls. When you enter Westminster after growing up in Birmingham, in an area where half the people are from an ethnic minority, it is another sharp shock. In my first week I expressed to a more seasoned MP my disquiet about how samey the staff drinking coffee in Portcullis House seemed. She joked, 'It's great if you don't know someone's name here; you can just guess at Will, Tom or Ben and you have a ninety per cent chance of being right.' On one occasion, a researcher for a fellow MP asked to meet me for a coffee in one of the cafés. I said, 'How will I know who you are?' in the hope that he was going to suggest he carry a carnation tucked into a copy of a great classic novel, à la rom-com blind-date scenario. He replied, 'I'm a twenty-five-year-old white man in a suit and a red tie.' Oh well, you'll stand out like a sore thumb here then, mate, I'll be able to spot you no trouble in the sea of culturally diverse women that usually fills up the tables in the coffee shops of Westminster.

In the whole time I've been at Westminster, I have seen only a handful of pregnant women. I've seen even fewer women wearing headscarves, and about three people in wheelchairs. The building itself speaks of a wholly uniform male era. In every room hang great portraits and in every corridor disembodied heads sit on plinths, while full-size statues loom eerily over proceedings. Aside from Margaret Thatcher and a few more modern portraits of Harriet Harman, Margaret Beckett and Diane Abbott (seemingly in the nude), the women depicted in these artworks seem to be either serving wenches or queens. There is little mention of the women in between.

In the secondary lobby area that leads from the vaulted and magnificent Central Lobby up to the committee rooms of Parliament are ornate carvings depicting both men and women as gargoyles. The men are depicted open-mouthed in speech; the women meanwhile are gagged, their mouths literally covered with stone muzzles. I have no idea if this was a less-than-subtle comment on gender equality by the architects of yesteryear, or a helpful suggestion. I hope it was the former, but sometimes I have my doubts. There are also charming little rooms dotted around the Palace entitled 'Lady Members' Rooms'. I kid you not, in some of these rooms you will find ironing boards, and glasses presented atop doilies. I've never been inside the men's rooms, but I'm fairly certain they are just bogs with no ironing facilities available. Aren't we the lucky ones? So far I've never had a crumpled clothes emergency, but when I do, I shall feel delighted that I can solve it in a jiffy.

If I dared to air these views on Twitter, you can bet that within seconds someone would shout, 'Meritocracy is what matters, not a person's gender or race.' Ah, meritocracy, that handy word (now so far departed from its origins) that cuts dead any talk of equality. The best person for the job is obviously always a white man; I suppose they are just better at everything. Oh, except the low-paid jobs like cleaning or caring. Funny how women, and even more so women of colour, are always the best people for these jobs. By funny, of course, I mean not funny at all. Really really not funny. The funny thing about those who demand a meritocracy is that they fail to recognise that no such thing has ever existed. Positive discrimination has been practised since the beginning of time, with men as the beneficiaries.

Theresa May, the new British prime minister, started her premiership with a strong emphasis on the idea of meritocracy. Selective education was her first attempt at making sure that those people who are better and cleverer are pushed to the front of the life lottery. I could spend pages and pages talking about what I wasn't keen on about my grammar school, if for no other reason than to annoy any Conservative readers of my book. I have learnt from Parliament that there are very few things that get Tory MPs salivating like the discussion about opening new selective schools. Grammar schools are to Conservative politicians what catnip is to cats. The fact that only 3 per cent of kids in these establishments are entitled to free school meals means I think the opposite. I think they are establishments with good intentions that are still for the haves rather than the have-nots.

Given her enthusiasm for meritocracy, I can only assume that Mrs May will soon roll out the policy of 100 per cent inheritance tax to make sure that people can't benefit from the spoils of their mummies and daddies. If we want meritocracy, I'm game; let's wipe the slate clean, stop anyone getting any advantage from birth or geography. Let's only judge people on exactly what they can deliver and pay them accordingly. No more House of Lords, no more Duchy of this or that, no more royal family. I suppose we could have a competition to decide who would make the best royal family; an *It's a Knockout*-style contest. Yeah, I'm liking this meritocracy idea. Not very bright rich kids could get exactly the same chances in life as not very bright poor kids. What's that, Theresa? You want to keep the House of Lords and the birth rite of Lord Snootlebury? You love the Queen, and you think people should pay less inheritance tax? Oh, and you don't think Prince Charles should have to prove he's the best man for the job in a race against the clock; he should just get it because he's the oldest boy? So you don't like meritocracy at all? Oh Teresa, I'm so confused.

Positive discrimination is a thorny subject. I have made no secret of the fact that I was selected on an all-women shortlist (AWS). People often use this to assert that I was not the best person for the job, merely the best woman. Because you know, women aren't people apparently. I wonder if Jessica Ennis-Hill was ever told this? 'Er, sorry, Jess, your Olympic gold medal isn't a real one because you only competed against other women; instead we've given you this medal we call girlie gold.'

Tory women are not fond of positive discrimination when it comes to selecting their candidates. Just as an aside, however, there is something they *are* really fond of, and that is shortening their first names to bullet-like single syllables. We have a Flick and a Mimms, and I bet you didn't know that Theresa or Therese is often shortened to Tizz. I'd never heard any of these names before entering Parliament. On hearing Therese Coffey referred to as Tizz, I decided I wanted a chippy short name too, except on reflection mine would be Jizz, which I think we can all agree is not a good look.

Anyway, back to positive discrimination. I have heard many a short-named Tory woman dismiss – or diss, as they might say – the idea of quotas in politics, and indeed in all industries. In some cases they even lord it over Labour women selected that way, as if they are superior because they fought against men. Bearing in mind that in the whole history of Parliament only 132 Tory women ever got there, and right now there are 101 Labour women MPs, I don't think they have any reason to gloat. One female Tory MP said to me, with some sadness, 'We couldn't have women-only elections because it would only add to an already long list of reasons why some of our male colleagues don't think we are good enough.' There is the rub: the idea that the women in Parliament are not as good as the men, and the women selected on all-women shortlists are even a rung below that. This is exactly the same for women working in other sectors. In every office and every factory there is someone who thinks that women are just not as good at the job. For many of the men in Parliament – and I am sure the country – my place in the House of Commons represents the lowest standard in the building. They think I only got there because I am a woman, when in actual fact I got there in spite of the fact that I am a woman.

In order to debunk the idea that women only get jobs through positive discrimination and are therefore not as good, we can simply have a quick comparison of the men and women in Parliament. If I had the time, I would invite you all in to see for yourselves; two minutes in the chamber would show you that there are some pretty amazing women (and men, of course) and some painfully mediocre men (and women). The best debunking of the mediocrity myth is in the recent US presidential race. Hillary Clinton, an educated and experienced stateswoman, versus Donald Trump, a man who as far as I can tell is a thick-as-two-short-planks shyster with no political experience at all who accused Hillary of 'playing the woman card'.

Edwina Currie said of women elected via AWS, 'Women who've come through this route have skipped several steps so their skills may be deficient.' Alas, Ms Currie, it's your analysis that is deficient, and I've got the evidence to prove it. Mary Nugent, a PhD candidate, and Mona Lena Krook, Associate Professor of Political Science at Rutgers University, collected data on the previous political experience of women elected to the UK Parliament via AWS compared to their non-quota counterparts, male and female, across the three main parties for every parliament from 1992 to 2010. They wrote:

We find that women elected by AWS were no less experienced than other MPs when they entered Parliament. In fact, women elected via AWS tend to have spent more time in a prior elected position than their Labour colleagues, male and female, in every year except 2010.

Interestingly, the data also show that AWS women had significantly more experience, on average, than Conservative MPs, male or female, in every parliament in this period. In 2010, for example, the mean years of prior experience of AWS women was 6.8 years, compared to 4.4 for Conservative men.

I'll be writing a little note to Theresa May to suggest she looks at quotas for Tory women when considering making the UK more meritocratic.

Although I am already clearly vindicated by the facts, one could argue that political experience doesn't cut it. So here is my completely non-scientific and probably biased analysis. I'm really not joking about the non-scientific bit. This is a comparison of what Wikipedia has to say about the experience of three pairs of MPs elected in 2005, 2010 and 2015: in each case, one woman selected using AWS, and an MP chosen by open selection.

Elected in 2005
    Philip Davies, Conservative Member of Parliament for Shipley (he would add hater of women's quotas if he could, I'm sure)

Davies studied at Huddersfield Polytechnic (which would become Huddersfield University in his third year), graduating in 1993 with a 2:1 BA (Hons) degree in history and political studies. He then worked at Asda until May 2005, as a customer services manager and, later, a marketing manager. He also worked at two bookmakers.

Roberta Blackman-Woods, Labour Member of Parliament for City of Durham (AWS)

Before becoming an MP, Blackman-Woods was an academic, serving as Dean of Social and Labour Studies at Ruskin College, Oxford, and, as a sociologist with expertise in housing, as Dean and Professor of Social Policy at the University of Northumbria. She was also a councillor in Newcastle and Oxford and head of policy at the Local Government Information Unit. Before this, she worked as a welfare rights officer for Newcastle City Council.

I think we can all agree that Roberta Blackman-Woods was pretty well qualified and goddamn expert and frankly brings an awful lot to the table in the way of experience that might be pretty good when discussing policy. Philip Davies would no doubt suggest he still deserved his place more than her because she was selected by AWS.

Elected in 2010

Valerie Vaz, Labour Member of Parliament for Walsall South (AWS)

After completing a biochemistry degree at Bedford College, University of London, Vaz qualified as a solicitor and then worked as a lawyer in local government. She set up a community law firm, Townsend Vaz Solicitors, and has sat as a deputy district judge. She joined the Government Legal Service in 2001, and has worked at the Treasury Solicitor's Department and the Ministry of Justice.

Mark Spencer, Conservative Member of Parliament for Sherwood

Prior to entering Parliament, Spencer studied at Shuttleworth Agricultural College in Bedfordshire and then joined the family farm business.

Both Vaz and Spencer were also elected to local government for similar periods of time before becoming MPs; even in that test Vaz did better, serving as deputy leader of her council while Mark only managed shadow spokesman for Community Safety Partnership. I'm not suggesting for a second that being a farmer means that you shouldn't be an MP, or that Spencer doesn't deserve his seat. I am merely pointing out that in terms of qualifications and experience, Vaz has him licked. But yeah, she had special treatment to get her there. Whatevs.

Finally, for balance, let's look at two female MPs elected on the same day.

Elected in 2015

Andrea Jenkyns, Conservative Member of Parliament for Morley and Outwood

Jenkyns graduated from the University of Lincoln with a degree in international relations and politics, and has a diploma in economics from the Open University. She has worked as a secondary school music teacher, an opera singer and as international business development manager for a management training company.

Jo Cox, Labour Member of Parliament for Batley and Spen (AWS)

Cox graduated from Pembroke College, Cambridge, with a BA in social and political science, and later studied at the London School of Economics. She spent a decade working for the aid agency Oxfam, first in Brussels as the leader of the group's trade reform campaign, then as head of policy and advocacy, and lastly as head of Oxfam International's humanitarian campaigns in New York City. She then worked as an adviser to Sarah Brown (the wife of former Prime Minister Gordon Brown), who was leading a campaign to stop mothers and babies dying in pregnancy and childbirth. She was the national chair of the Labour Women's Network and a senior adviser to the Freedom Fund, an anti-slavery charity. Before her death, Cox was also trying to launch UK Women, a research institute dedicated to better understanding the needs of women in the UK. She was nominated in 2009 by the Davos

World Economic Forum as a young global leader, and in 2012 received the DEVEX award for her contribution to international development.

Take that, naysayers about women elected on AWS. Positive discrimination delivers absolutely kick-ass women to the UK Parliament. Women who have managed to fit in being lawyers, biochemists and mothers. Women who have been internationally recognised as peacekeepers and scholars. Women who came from ordinary backgrounds and rose to be massively respected in their fields of academia, international development and law. Highly educated women, women with amazing work and life experience. There is absolutely no evidence that women selected using positive discrimination shouldn't be there or are less qualified. Both the numbers and the narrative prove this. (If you still don't believe me, I suggest you spend even one hour watching Philip Davies in Parliament and compare him to Caroline Flint, Yvette Cooper, Mary Creagh, Shabana Mahmood or Alison McGovern. I think the reason he hates positive discrimination so much is because it delivers women who make him look mediocre at best.)

Positive discrimination and quotas have very few examples in the real world outside politics. Only in recent years has there been a push for big businesses to have women on their boards, or for them to publish their equal pay analysis. In most everyday women's lives there is no quota system to propel them forward. I think the argument for how this tinkering improves meritocracy is won, and I would push for it across the board in all industries. Time will tell if the evidence from big business quotas will support my case.

While positive discrimination does not exist in most workplaces, the idea that women do better or go further because they are women is alive and well everywhere. In every job I've ever had since becoming a mother, I was made to feel by both male and female colleagues that I was given special treatment because I had children. When my mother was dying and I needed time to care for her, I felt as if some colleagues thought it was unfair that I was given flexibility to help me cope. I've read article after article by shoulder-padded female execs saying things like, 'If you want to be taken seriously, don't moan about your kids at work, or show emotion in the boardroom.' Whenever women are promoted over men, it is met with snide political-correctness gags.

This resistance to positive discrimination might not be stated directly in the workplace, but it certainly exists. The reality of course is that no one bats an eyelid if a man is promoted above a woman or gets a job because of the old-boy network. If a man asks for time off to go to his kid's play or pick up his relative from the hospital, in most cases he isn't considered to be getting special treatment; people simply say what a good family man he is. I call on everyone to use the same rules across the board. Roll your eyes and insist that Malcolm got the job over Susan just because he is a man. (It is much more likely to be true.) When Mark and Pete have to swap shifts so Mark can look after the kids, insist that Mark is getting special treatment just because he is a dad. If we are going to be narky (which we shouldn't be) about parents in the workplace, can we at least be consistent?

The Labour Party should be praised not vilified for their attempts at positive discrimination. We have the body-count issue sorted: we have found a way of increasing the numbers of women that is actually more meritocratic than less. We can pat ourselves on the back that of all the women who have ever sat in the UK Parliament, 58 per cent of them were from the Labour Party. That is where we must stop our self-praise. If my nan were still alive, she would tell the Labour Party to stand in the corner and have a word with itself. UKIP had a female leader. UKIP! Yes, the populist right-wing party famous for a man who said that women who don't clean behind the fridge are sluts. They have smashed the glass ceiling that the Labour Party has failed to come close to. Obviously Diane James did only last eighteen days in the role, and it turns out that she wrote (in Latin) on her leadership registration papers, 'under duress', which is one of the most sinister and bizarre examples of positive discrimination I've ever heard of. It appears that she was literally forced to do it, in what seems like a *Game of Thrones*-style power play by some of the men. Not cool, dudes, and I'm not here to suggest that this is somehow the solution to the problem. However, the fact still stands: UKIP elected a female leader. Pundits ask me often if I would like to be the leader of the Labour Party, and at the moment the answer is simply that there is absolutely no chance. I was born a girl child. While it's very nice to have been heralded by some as a candidate, I still think that the party – despite appearances – isn't ready for a female leader.

Scott Taylor, a reader in leadership and organisation studies at the University of Birmingham, and Owain Smolovic Jones, a lecturer in organisation studies at the Open University, have argued that while gender quotas are successful in increasing women's representation, they do not change sexism in an organisation. In their article 'Why Gender Quotas in Business and Politics Are Ineffective in Overcoming Sexism' they state: 'All the organisational research tells us very clearly that deep-rooted patterns of "how things are done around here" are key to whether a workplace is hostile or welcoming to people who don't fit the white male norm. And underlying an organisation's culture is its sense of identity.'

This is exactly the problem that the Labour Party has, a problem shared by companies and employers everywhere. Its identity is so steeped in the idea of the class struggle between the haves and the have-nots that it often cannot see past the end of its currently very bloody nose. Women are still considered as window-dressing. The fight for wage equality between rich and poor is the long-held struggle of the party; while noble, this simply lumps women in the poor column and fails to grasp the intersectional issues of gender. It also fails to recognise that women organising together and acting as leaders could be the solution to this struggle for all, instead of just the solution to the problem for other women.

Outside of Westminster, we have a defined idea of women's jobs and men's jobs. Men take on dirty, tough roles, while women hold more caring employment. The culture of men as train drivers and women as nurses, for example, needs to be stamped out. Women are no more caring than men; men are no more capable of engineering. Men don't want caring jobs, because when they close their eyes they see a woman in that role; likewise, women don't imagine female airline pilots or bridge builders. The definition of roles is straight out of a 1950s playbook, and we have got to undo that.

Prior to the 2015 election, I attended one of the regular Labour Party briefings for parliamentary candidates in London. One of the male MPs at the heart of the election campaign strategy team stood up to talk through charts and targets. As he ran through a list of the MPs in his team, only one woman's name came up. I raised my hand and questioned why in a team of eight or so people, only one was female. He snapped back at me, 'The Labour Party has a mountain to climb in winning men's votes. If as many men voted Labour as women did, we would win the election.' To which I replied, 'Are you suggesting that a woman can't be part of a team that wins men's votes?' Clearly I, as a woman, couldn't speak to the concerns of working-class men, businessmen, young men or old men. Instead I was there to have my photo taken with one of my babies on my hip to remind female voters that Labour loves women. The party of workers seems to have failed to notice that over the past hundred years – and in fact for all the centuries before that – women have been workers too. Our needs and hopes and our ability to communicate with our brothers in arms is not bleeding rocket science. I'm married to a man who drives a van, had a manual job and reads the tabloid press, but apparently I know nothing about men's lives; obviously I have been failing to talk to and understand him for the past ten years as far as Labour Party strategists are concerned.

A woman in Jeremy Corbyn's team once sent me a message about her frustrations with the leadership's approach to gender equality, saying, 'The current power adviser(s) of the left basically learnt their politics through the prism of class during their early political formation and questions such as equality are add-ons rather than core.' My problem with the Labour Party's current approach is that I think the leadership looks down on women as a group of patronised poor people who need the big important clever men to come and save them. Women's equality makes good copy when talking about pay and/or domestic violence, but when they close their eyes and think of great leaders, bold innovators or original thinkers, I bet all the tea in China that some bloke pops into their heads.

It is the very core identity of the Labour Party as the

party of the workers that holds it back when considering women. The identity of so many of our industries does the exact same thing. In the City, the image of slick young go-getting men working and partying hard, followed around by beautiful female assistants in fuck-me heels, runs deep, while mention of heavy manufacturing organisations brings to mind men in overalls, grafting and drinking strong tea. In every lab in the country women are working away on innovation that will save lives or make our phones charge faster for longer, but still science and tech is dominated by a bygone era of men with wild hair. Our national identity is still wedded to some imperial claptrap of Britain ruling the waves and being forged by dirty men while great engineers look on in their top hats and tails.

At the 2016 Labour Party conference Jeremy Corbyn did that really annoying and contrived thing where he walked over to the conference centre to give his speech surrounded by a crowd of women. Politicians of all stripes stage this performance for the media. Hell, I've been one of the people drafted in to walk that path myself in the days of Ed Miliband. Two of the best activists in my election campaign were constantly called away from the real job of campaigning in order to walk a hundred yards with a politician to make them look popular and attractive to a diverse audience. The fact that pretty much all UK party leaders in the past have been white men means that very often young, ethnically diverse women have to act as their chaperones. No doubt all over the world young women are receiving the call from their party asking if they can drop everything to stride meaningfully alongside a figurehead. I think it is naff, but then again they might look a bit lonely walking all by themselves.

Jeremy Corbyn was flanked by eight women as he walked the hundred yards to give his conference speech. It was designed to send a message: 'See, I don't have a woman problem. Please try to forget that time when I gave all the top jobs in my shadow cabinet to men. Look, all my friends are women.' Except what I saw was a tick box, a stunt, arm candy. What it screamed to me was the exact opposite: 'Look how bad the Labour Party's woman problem is.' Seriously, I don't think the suffragettes starved themselves in prison cells so that male politicians could one day look good with a crowd of women. Rather than feeling honoured to have been picked to accompany a man on stage, this particular group of women should have got together, had a chat and refused to walk anywhere unless they were guaranteed that Jeremy would ensure his shadow cabinet was 50 per cent female, or that he would make every Labour seat an AWS until at least half of Labour MPs were women. Every female Tory candidate who was called in to walk next to David Cameron during the election campaign should have refused to do it unless he promised to appoint a woman to be chancellor. Instead what they did – and I know, because I did it too – was turn up dutifully, grateful to be asked to make their men look good. There was literally nothing in it for them, but still they were just happy to be there. Excuse me while I smash my head against the wall for a few moments.

OK, I'm back, with a sore head and no further forward in the fight against being the token woman. There is a growing demand for women to be visible in public life. There is a growing demand for women to be visible in business and industries across the world. It is starting to be embarrassing if a company or a political party puts up a picture of a load of blokes in suits. TV panel shows and news programmes have been called out and criticised if they don't put women on their programmes. If you are reading this book, you are probably a right-on sort, so give yourself a pat on the back, because *we* did that. We, the good forward thinkers of the world, got off our arses and demanded to see something better. We must keep it up. Whenever we see a load of dudes running the world, we must post the pictures on social media, write letters of complaint, send it out to the world with the quick and easy hashtag #everydaysexism. Thanks to bold women like Laura Bates and her mighty hashtag, this is a battle we are winning, but we must keep up the pressure.

Every time I visit a business in my constituency I say, 'Where are the women?' Every group that lobbies me I ask, 'How many women are involved and what are the pay scales of these women?' When I visit mosques, churches, schools and community events, I refuse to be the only woman in the picture, and now, as a matter of course, I refuse to attend events unless there are going to be other women there. Never again will I allow people to take my photo flanked only by men. I know it really annoys people, but it makes them stop and think that they need to get more women involved with whatever they are doing. Image matters in a world where everyone is watching everything.

So the next stage of this plan is for the women who are drafted in for show to start making demands in return for their cooperation. If your manager wants you in a photo for the company brochure or wants to put you on the business's Facebook page, ask them what they are doing about the ratio of women to men in the top jobs. Ask them what plans they have to recruit, train or develop black and minority ethnic staff. Ask them what they are doing to provide flexibility in the workplace for staff with caring responsibilities. Hell, ask them, 'What's in it for me?' We have done the grunt work of shaming everyone for looking male, pale and stale. They need us now, so let's stop turning up dutifully to make them look good and start saying, 'No, Jeremy Corbyn, my sisters and I will not walk around with you making you look all woman-friendly, not unless you bloody well publish an equal pay audit of your office staff that bloody well proves to us we are not just window dressing.'

My advice to the women of the world is to leave this moment of gumption until the very last minute. People constantly roll their eyes at me when I demand they make sure women have been invited to their events and are in their pictures, but they are learning that if they want their ribbon cut, if they want me to fight their corner, they bloody well have to fight mine too. By all means be the token woman at an event, be the bit of colour in the line-up of grey, but make sure you speak up against your tokenism.

At the very same Labour conference where Jeremy Corbyn was adorned with young, ethnically diverse women, I sat in a very cold hotel room with him and told him that I was willing to do all I could to make him look good, I was willing to organise events for women and roll him out, I was willing to help boost his feminist credentials, but only if he guaranteed me a 50/50 cabinet, with women represented equally in every stratum of his shadow ministerial team. I told him I would look out for areas where he was going wrong and try to get in front of them rather than criticising the howling sexist gaffes afterwards. I made a promise to help him with his image, but I bloody well demanded he did stuff for Labour women too. If he does, I will sing his praises. If he doesn't, I shall make sure everybody knows it. In a world where how you appear matters so much, we women have got to wake up to the fact that they need us more than we need them. We must sweat our assets; let's go full-on Tyra Banks and get finger-snapping demanding.

Someone very wise yet not great at PR once said (in an unattributed quote), 'When you're accustomed to privilege, equality feels like oppression.' This is the eloquent version of 'Check your privilege.' We must all keep saying this. We have got to move the pervading identity of power away from always being in the image of a man in a suit. No matter how oppressed that makes the privileged feel. If it means forcing the issue with quotas and PR stunts, then that is what we should do. It works, it has been working for decades, and slowly but surely things are improving so that ignoring women's voices is becoming embarrassing. 'Sausage fest!' was shrieked at the Birmingham Local Enterprise Partnership's publicity image, which featured twenty men and one woman; the next photo I saw of the group had a more diverse make-up. Each week now on *Question Time*, or *Have I Got News For You*, there is always at least one woman in the line-up, after years of us all sending sarky emails and comments. Those who complain about positive discrimination, those who indignantly yell 'Meritocracy!' at us from the sidelines do it because it is working. We have got to stop listening to those voices; we have got to stop feeling guilty about demanding our seat on a panel, our place in management. We have got to believe that we got where we are because we are good, not because we might have been given a little hand up to counteract the enormous fist pushing us down.

I am not grateful to the quota system that meant I made it to Parliament; I bloody well deserve to be there. Frankly, I'm annoyed that it still has to exist for people like me to get a chance. If people are pissed off with the system for getting talented women into Parliament or on to management boards, then it's because they just plain and simple don't think women are good enough to be there. Let's stop trying to find a way of making these people come along with us, and call them what they are: ignorant sexists. Let's take off our tiny stone-carved muzzles and talk over them in meetings, just like they've always done to us.

THE TRUTH ABOUT
VIOLENCE

When I left the bubble of women's services to go to Westminster, I wanted to be a voice for the abused in Parliament. I think I'm giving it my best shot, but I'm struck every day by how much we all still turn a blind eye to a horror that is so prolific. Where I live, a domestic violence incident is reported to West Midlands Police every twelve seconds. In 2016, a woman was murdered in the UK every three days. The number of sexual offences recorded in 2015 was the highest ever. Yet the number of emails I have had lobbying for women's services is six; the number I have had about child abuse: eight. In the same period, I have had ninety emails about bees, 324 about foxes, seventeen about dog meat and twenty-five about dog fighting.

People really care about animals and they want to tell their MP about it. The actual number of animal-welfare-related incidents I have dealt with as an MP is four. On one bizarre occasion, a woman had found a false black widow spider in her house and wanted to offer it up for scientific efforts to find a vaccine. The number of victims of domestic violence and child abuse I have helped runs into the hundreds. The demand for this support is so high that once a week Birmingham and Solihull Women's Aid places a specialist domestic abuse support worker in my office to help arrange appointments. So far my one false black widow spider has not led me to need a specialist arachnid expert. So why is it that I am lobbied so hard about animals and so rarely about women?

The amount of money given in charitable donations every year in the UK to donkeys is more than the amount donated to women's charities. In 2008, the New Philanthropy Capital undertook a study of what the British public was giving its money to; a sort of whose tin rattles loudest. They found that Refuge, the Women's Aid Federation, and Eaves Housing for Women had a combined annual income of just £17m. By contrast, a donkey sanctuary in Devon received £20m in one year. I've no idea how many donkeys there are in the UK; I rarely see them on the bus or down the local pub, so I'm guessing they are outnumbered by women. The money being donated to donkeys leads me to believe that they are well rich; get yourself a donkey, you'll be quids in. Maybe they have very expensive tastes and need to be bathed in Evian; perhaps they have a penchant for oysters and holidays in the French Riviera. I suppose they deserve an exclusive break after schlepping up and down Blackpool beach from March to September. The seven million women abused in a year would be lucky to get a stick of rock.

I like donkeys as much as the next person, but I don't think they should get more money than women and children who have been beaten, abused, raped or tortured. On one occasion, when I was expressing my exasperation about the donkeys-to-women financial ratio to my mate Ruth, she said, 'To be fair, I've never met a donkey I didn't like.' While she was clearly joking, I think she was actually on to something. As a society, we are not that keen on women who have been victims of domestic and sexual violence. 'She was asking for it' is alive and well and happening on a street near you.

I have a fancy job now, one of the fanciest you can have. They literally film me doing my job every day so people can watch the fanciness. People take photos of where I work, and you can buy a key ring or a mug with a picture of my office on it. However, the most important, most life-changing job I ever had was working at Sandwell Women's Aid with victims of domestic and sexual violence, human trafficking and slavery.

People always comment that my old job must have been terribly difficult. Many times they have poured sympathy over me for the things they imagine I have seen and heard. In reality, it was a happy place to work. I only ever cried twice while working at Women's Aid. One time over the case of a young woman whose ex-boyfriend would arrive every Friday night to rape her, sometimes bringing his friends. She wouldn't tell me her address or her full name; she just wanted to talk. I begged her to tell the police or to let me turn up and stop it happening. So used to her abuse was she, so sure that her boyfriend would never be convicted or stopped, that she had learned to live with it. I thought about her every Friday night for weeks and weeks, weeping at my inability to help her. On another occasion I took a referral over the phone and immediately threw up with horror. The case concerned two brothers who were the exact ages of my sons at the time: three and seven. Their story is too sensitive to repeat, but I remember sleeping alongside my children in their room for a good week after hearing it. So of course I have heard terrible things, stories that would make your blood boil and your heart sink, but the truth is that mostly it was an utterly amazing place to work, full of genuine belly laughs, cups of tea, and extraordinary and inspiring characters.

Compared to Westminster, Women's Aid was a barrel of laughs and a place full of love. I suppose that is the difference between working somewhere based on competition and opposition and working in a place designed for kindness.

People often ask me how I got involved in working in that field, and I'm afraid it's no great story: the truth is I just applied for a job. Sandwell is a small borough no one has ever heard of in the Black Country in the West Midlands. The charity was small, and in 2009, when I joined, it was facing financial difficulties as austerity was beginning to bite. I had always wanted to work with victims of domestic violence. I was raised by feminists to be a feminist. While I was having my own babies and was off work I had done a number of voluntary jobs. One of these – my favourite – had involved working with refugee women. When the job at Sandwell came up, I thought I had something to offer them. This was potentially delusional, as I had never worked in the field other than one afternoon a week at stay-and-plays, always with one of my own children clamped on my hip. I was hardly support worker of the year.

I applied for the job as a sort of PA to the director. The person they originally wanted had turned it down, so it came to me. Bear in mind that this was only seven years ago. I was the second choice for a low-level job in a small local charity in a place no one had heard of. Today I am probably one of the go-to voices in the world on the issue of violence against women. In March 2016 I addressed a congress at the UN in New York on the subject, on the same platform as Madeleine Albright, the first woman to become American Secretary of State. I literally went from writing emails in an office in West Bromwich to being written about in the *New York Times*. That's what being delusional, giving a toss about something, and a willingness to speak up can do.

While at Women's Aid, I worked with a core team of five amazing – if slightly quirky – female managers who taught me that self-ambition is nothing compared to the ambition to build something for other people. These women are absolute giants, amazing businesswomen and pre-eminent in their fields of psychotherapy or social work, but if a bed needed to be built or a chip-pan fire needed putting out in one of the refuge flats, they would be the first to roll up their sleeves. I look at them now winning awards and changing the world and I giggle at the memories of us all trying to erect IKEA furniture, or making hundreds of baps for the buffet at a conference we had organised.

I think back to the hours of interviewing for new support workers and trying to keep a straight face when candidates said things like 'I've proven my commitment to human and women's rights by becoming a vegetarian.' Great stuff, love, I'll inform the women that they're not at risk of you eating them. Or the time when we were interviewing for an Asian women's support worker required to have a community language. During the obligatory language test one candidate just pretended that she could speak Punjabi, literally speaking gobbledygook in response to the questions. I think of all the times when we would drop our plans for the evening because inevitably a woman and her three kids would rock up with their stuff in black bin bags at bang on 4.55 on a Friday afternoon. The lives of the women who worked there were as important as the lives of the service users. This was a place that was about getting a better deal for all the women involved and putting up with the sacrifices that might be required to make that happen.

In my time at Women's Aid, we opened seven new refuge sites, giving a home to hundreds of women and children fleeing violence; we opened new rape crisis centres, created specialist services for children who had been sexually abused or exploited, set up a service for victims of human trafficking and slavery, and opened two shiny new specialist centres for vulnerable female offenders. Like I said, when I started there, the charity was in trouble: 50 per cent of the core funding was at risk and some had already gone. Together we had to completely rethink how the organisation had worked in the past. I was raised on the principle that the state should pay for all services. I still believe that with every fibre of my being. But believing it won't make it happen. You can join as many protests as you like – and believe me, I do – but ultimately we had to find a new way of doing things. When I left Sandwell Women's Aid to go to Westminster, the charity had trebled its income and its number of staff; it had gone from having three bases in one borough to ten bases across the West Midlands. It had national contracts with the government and was regularly called upon to take an advisory role at the Ministry of Justice and the Home Office.

When I stepped up to be a politician, it was because I really thought that my experience at Women's Aid meant I had something to offer the country. I wanted to scream to the world about what I had seen and demand solutions. I believe I have a place I can lead people to and it is a place worth going. I carry with me every victim I met or developed services for, and in my time at Women's Aid this was over 10,000 people.

We think we have come far from the idea that 'she was asking for it', but we haven't at all. To be fair, it is now more commonly rephrased as 'Why doesn't she leave?' The meaning is the same: the intention is to blame the woman involved. The question of course should be 'Why does he beat his wife?' Or 'Why did he rape her?' Every day, up and down the country, people fail to compute why a woman stays in an abusive relationship. This has nothing to do with knowledge and understanding; it is entirely to do with projecting our own fears and discomfort on to a situation that has absolutely nothing to do with us. We are so desperate to convince ourselves that this would never happen to us, we have to diminish the credibility of the person it does happen to in order to feel safe.

It's a bit like when someone has suffered a bereavement and a well-wisher doesn't know what to say to them, so reaches for a kindly platitude. 'Everything happens for a reason' is the absolute classic. When my mom died, I heard a lot of 'She's gone to a better place.' On one occasion my kids were told that she was on a star – this obviously begged the question 'Why doesn't she come and visit us from the star, Mommy?' When bad things happen, people struggle to accept it; they have to find a way of dealing with it. Our attitude to domestic violence is exactly the same, and alas, this perpetuates a culture of victim-blaming by people who would identify themselves as reasonable, good-minded souls who hate and abhor violence against women.

As an aide-memoir, here is my handy guide to why she doesn't leave.

She is terrified about what will happen to her if she does

While working in the field of violence against women, I sat in on many domestic homicide reviews. This is a process of scrutiny for public services (police, NHS, social services) that happens after a person is murdered by a member of their family or someone they live in a domestic setting with. The vast majority of domestic homicide reviews that take place in the UK involve a woman murdered by her partner. If we look back over all these reviews, there are not many trends that can be identified. Murdered women come from every socio-economic background; no race or religion murders more than another. Perpetrators range in age from eighteen to eighty and come from varied backgrounds, with no job type or character trait standing out. The only thing that comes up time and time again, the only recurring theme, is that the murder so often took place after the woman finally made the break to be free.

If someone has abused you to the point that you have to be rescued from them, the likelihood is they are the controlling type. Once the woman has left and the perpetrator has lost control, the perpetrator's actions are unpredictable, dangerous and, in too many cases I have dealt with, fatal. We have all heard the stories about a man who murders his wife and kids with the romanticised idea of 'If I can't have them, no one can.' We spend our time urging women to leave for their own safety, whereas in reality, many know that leaving, without support, will put them at greater risk than staying. If I had a pound for every woman I've met who said when I urged her to leave, 'You don't understand, he will kill me if I go . . .' I'm in no way encouraging people to stay in violent relationships; I'm just saying I get it. I understand that women who live in violent or abusive situations often become amazing at managing their own risk. Unless a woman can access genuinely safe support or secure an easy and quick conviction against her abuser (ha ha ha), leaving is a very real and present danger.

She will lose everything

Imagine you are sat in your office or having a cuppa in a café. The fire alarm starts to sound and helpful people with high-vis tabards start to usher you towards the exit. What do you do? Do you (a) drop everything and dash to the nearest exit, or (b) pick up your phone, your bag, maybe your coat, perhaps even the paper you were in the middle of reading, because after all, you might be left standing outside in a car park for a bit while this whole annoying rigmarole is going on and fancy having something to do while you're waiting?

If you answered (a), you are lying to yourself. Everyone

in the world picks up their phone at least. When threatened with the possibility of danger, we would still rather take a few seconds, which could potentially be a life-threatening margin of error, to ensure that we have our iPhone. Yet when we utter the words 'Why doesn't she leave?' we expect women to literally pick themselves up one day and leave behind their homes, their hopes, their dreams, their shoes, clothes, income, friends, family and – in the most heartbreaking cases – their children. For many women, walking away from domestic violence means that they lose everything they ever had. For some it is a price worth paying, but don't for a second think it is an easy decision to make. After all, we've all risked our safety to stop and pick up our phone, just so we can play Candy Crush while waiting for the fire alarm all-clear.

She will have her children taken away from her

Every day there are women who stay put because they have been told that if they speak up, go to a refuge or ask for help, social services will come along and take their children. This is a tactic used by perpetrators to great effect. Women are also told how their perpetrator will win custody of the kids and they will never be free of him. I am afraid to say that at the moment the state colludes with this idea. I have met hundreds of women who were sent on courses by social services because their husband beat them. Women are told over and over that they can't keep their children safe and are blamed for what is happening to them by a system that offers them little in the way of support. If you call the police and tell the truth, chances are a social worker will be assigned to you. This terrifies women who would do anything to stay close to their children. Of course for many, social services can be a gateway to support and freedom but ask yourself this: if you thought someone was going to question whether your kids were safe with you, would you speak up?

She cannot see her situation as violent; it is just her life

In the refuge where I used to work, there was a woman who would come in around Christmas time for respite. She was an elderly Irish woman who had been married for decades to a man she loved and was committed to. He used to bash her about, and as far as I could see she had a fairly traditional sort of role where she was essentially his maid. She would never have considered leaving him, and we would never have pushed her to, but we were there if she needed a break from it. This is the case for lots of women. They have learnt to tolerate and accept their abuse as part of the normal pattern of their lives. We all do it. We all diminish the bad stuff that happens to us. It is how we cope and we shouldn't ever judge how others get by.

Next time you hear someone ask why a woman stays, why she didn't leave, I ask you to pull out one of these handy answers. Apply even one of them to your own life and tell me with certainty that you would leave. We have got to stop judging women for staying in abusive relationships. I will support women whether they leave, stay or can't make up their minds. The question should never be 'Why does she stay?' or comments like 'Blimey, she can't half pick them!' It should always be 'What can I do to support her, even if she is never going to leave?'

Before everyone shouts at once, I know domestic violence happens to men too. I have been to hundreds of meetings and events about domestic violence. In every single meeting without fail, someone stands up and thinks they are utterly righteous and original when they announce that men are also victims of domestic violence. In every funding meeting someone raises the question 'What money are we putting into men's services?' So let's get over this: yes I know it happens to men as well, I worked at a service that offered support to male victims of domestic and sexual violence. I've done more to try and help male victims of violence than pretty much all of those people who assume I don't give a damn.

In domestic violence services only a handful of men ever came forward for support, and they received it. As far as I can remember, no man ever asked for refuge. During my time at our completely non-gendered sexual violence service, around 8 per cent of victims we worked with were male; they had almost exclusively been abused or assaulted by other men. There is a statistic from the British Crime Survey doing the rounds that suggests that one in three domestic violence incidents has a man as the victim. It is completely misleading, but my God do politicians desperate to show they know their onions like to quote it. I was in a meeting at the UN when a British male politician said, 'Of course we know half of domestic violence victims are men.' Wrong. Completely and utterly wrong. The British Crime Survey contrasts significantly with data from police crime reports, which estimate that between 80 and 90 per cent of reported violence is by men assaulting women.

I do care about men who suffer domestic and sexual violence and I want to help them, but I am sick of how politicians and the noisy ill-informed constantly seek to undermine the fact that the vast majority of interpersonal violence is against women and children. It is a gendered crime. End of. I am tired of people complaining about the lack of services for men but never piping up about the fact that there are almost no special services for older women, disabled women or women with learning difficulties. These are areas that really need a champion. It is almost as if people feel the need to say 'It happens to men too' to diminish the fact that violence happens to women because we have a lower position in society.

Also, as it happens to men too, I would invite all those who care so much about that, the ones who make such a fuss about it, to create a movement, prove the need and demand and get funding and support for your services. I'll gladly come and cut the ribbon on your refuge or support centre. I will delight in your success, I'll be the first at the celebratory buffet. Goddammit, I'll probably even help you fill in your forms and get you the backing you need. Crack on with it, but don't ring up Women's Aid and talk about men, just like you wouldn't ring up Cats Protection and say, 'I've got this sick parrot, can you help?'

While we struggle to compute what it means to be a victim of gendered violence in the home, we do love a tale of a survivor. When working with victims of abuse, the politically correct and empowering way to describe your service users is as 'survivors'. It is usually a phrase reserved for those who are now free from harm. I think it is a nice sentiment but I worry that it often excludes the women still living every day under tyranny. These women feel weak, hopeless, worthless and alone, but in my experience they are some of the strongest and bravest people I have ever met.

Lucy (not her real name) was sitting in the waiting room at Sandwell Women's Aid when I went for my interview. She was seventeen years old and not very talkative, in that way that seventeen-year-old girls aren't. I could never have mistaken her for a fellow candidate for the job; she looked more like a sullen twelve-year-old, in a dirty sweatshirt and jogging bottoms, as she sat there awaiting her support worker. After I got the job, I saw Lucy many more times; she visited almost every week, sometimes more frequently. From the age of five until she was around twelve, she had been abused by her grandfather. She originally came to the service to receive support with court proceedings and her emotional well-being. She had been in and out of the care system her whole childhood and had fractured relations with her mother, who on one occasion set fire to the house while Lucy was inside. As a teenager, Lucy's level of vulnerability, naivety and self-destruction had led her into the arms of men who had exploited her further, selling her to other people for sex and feeding her drugs to control her.

As you read this, I can feel your heart breaking for Lucy. She is so obviously a victim: an innocent child left with no chances in life, abused by nearly every adult she ever trusted. You would think that we live in a comfortable, kind society that would look after children who have suffered these horrors. You probably feel like you would want to give Lucy a cuddle. The reality is, of course, quite different. Our justice system, largely run by men, doesn't see a victim in front of them. We've all walked past the Lucys of the world and judged. Helping someone like Lucy is hard: she absconds, she smokes heroin in the refuge, she kicks the doors down, she doesn't ever keep an appointment but always turns up just when you can't manage her needs. I remember one brilliant occasion when she asked to use the phone in reception to call the Job Centre, and I walked back into the room to find her at our public reception desk carrying out a very obvious drug deal.

Lucy is exactly the kind of girl who doesn't get justice for the abuse she has suffered. The world sees women like her as common, scroungers, criminals, sluts. She is not a picture-postcard survivor, someone who came back from the brink and is now achieving it all, but she is one of the greatest survivors I've ever encountered. She is surviving by selling herself to men, hustling for her life, doing things that harm her, yes – but just imagine waking up every day having lived that life. Actually having the energy to raise your head off the pillow on whichever floor you slept on last night and carry on. This is a survival most of us cannot even comprehend. And because we can't comprehend it, it is easier for us to think ill of Lucy, that it must have been her fault. Like so many women and girls, she was asking for it, or so says society and our own common view.

We are wrong to think that the abuse women suffer is always physical or sexual. Some of the worst and most terrifying abuse I have seen involved no violence at all. I spoke to one woman who had met a man and given up her job to move away with him. She fell pregnant quite early on in the relationship and was looking forward to their life together. Her partner had bought a house for them to share and convinced her she didn't need to work, and who was going to employ a woman who was pregnant anyway? One day he took her to the new house and left her there, locking her in and telling her to clean it, and that he would pick her up on his way home from work. He did exactly the same the next day, and the next day, and the next. He kept promising they would be moving to the new house soon. By the time I met her, months had passed and she was now heavily pregnant. She had no money or access to any benefits. Every day would end with her partner inspecting her cleaning efforts. He never raised his hand to her, never beat her or raped her. He controlled her, isolated and diminished her, and she had no one but him to turn to. This treatment was just as menacing and terrifying as physical or sexual abuse, and even harder for people to comprehend.

Domestic violence happens to posh women too. I have met women who live in mansions that have become their prisons. Women who don't depend on benefits or haven't had a run-in with social services rarely see themselves as victims. One woman I met had a six-bedroom home on the coast, was part of her community and envied on the school run. Her husband had abused her mentally and physically for twenty-seven years. Even after he had raped her so brutally as to cause her a spinal injury, she still did not think of herself as being like 'one of those women'. It is usually when violent men turn on their children that women finally see the harm they have caused.

I'm worried that I am bumming you out. My cynicism comes from the hundreds and hundreds of cases where I have seen victims badly let down, told by the police that the courts will take no further action, told by the housing department that there is nowhere for them to go, or deported back to a country where their lives are at risk. I don't want for a second for anyone to think that women shouldn't leave or that no support exists. It is available, and eventually even those in the worst situations can break free and rebuild themselves and their families.

Some of the most hopeful and inspiring cases I came across in our refuge were victims of human trafficking. Most of the women who lived in the refuge had been trafficked for sex or had been sold into servitude as slaves in businesses, restaurants or even fancy homes. While many people cannot compute the evils of domestic violence, human trafficking designed to make money out of misery is even more incomprehensible, yet in the UK every year thousands of people are sold into slavery. The women and men I met were usually left living in squalor, sleeping in shifts, never with a bed to call their own. They were allowed to sleep only until their time to have sex with the next punter or clean the next room came up.

One woman, Anna, would sleep on the floor or on the sofa in the refuge's living room, so conditioned was she to not having a bed. Her support worker, Chereene, caught her doing it a few times and had to coax her to sleep in her bedroom. I interviewed Anna for a piece of work I was doing for the Home Office and she laughed when I asked her about the bed. Swearing me to secrecy, she told me that she still slept on the sofa and set an alarm so that she would wake before Chereene arrived in the morning, then mess up her bed as if she had been sleeping in it to fool her, Ferris Bueller style. She was highly amused by her ruse. When I asked her why she didn't want to sleep in her bed she answered that she had never in all her life had a room of her own or a bed of her own and she couldn't get used to it. She said she was certain she didn't deserve it. Weeks of therapy and support later, she left the refuge ready to start a new life. She asked if she could take a copy of her room key to remind her that she had a place in the world and that she deserved it.

I have worked with women who have the most horrific tales to tell and I have tried to spend my time in Parliament giving voice to these stories. I have given accounts of rape as a weapon of war, told stories of lives of torture and fear. These big, terrifying stories exist, but the reality of violence against women is far less bombastic, far more pedestrian. It is the stuff that happens to pretty much every woman I have ever met that people find hardest to believe.

The unpalatable truth is that women are sexually harassed and assaulted hundreds and hundreds of times every day in this country, and always have been. When I spoke about this on *Question Time*, I received countless messages from women telling me about things that had happened to them, but also letters from men sharing the experiences of their daughters, sisters and wives. Violence against women is not something that just happens on a TV drama or in one section of society: it is everywhere. These are my own experiences:

When I was thirteen, I was waiting outside my mate Jess's house while she got ready. I was in my school uniform. A man pulled up in a car and asked me if I was working; at the time I had no clue what he meant, but I realise now he thought I was a prostitute. He asked me to get in the car. I declined, so he sat in front of me and began to masturbate. I was terrified.

At fourteen, I was in the park with a big bunch of mates, boys and girls. A group of lads approached us, dragged one of my mates into the bushes and sexually assaulted her. They beat up one of the lads, too. When we left the park, a police car happened to be passing so we flagged it down and asked for help. They simply treated us like a group of drunk kids.

At sixteen, a bunch of my mates and I went away to Cornwall for a camping trip. My mate was chatting with a bloke and they disappeared together for a bit, so we went looking for her. She returned a while later, having managed to escape after he had dragged her into the back of a van and tried to have sex with her.

When I was nineteen and having a drink in a bar, I got chatting to some blokes. One of them pinned me against a wall and stuck his hand up my skirt and inside my knickers in full view of his mates. I slapped him in the face and was thrown out of the bar, even though I told the security staff what had happened. The man and his mates laughed at me as I was ejected.

And these are a few of the hundreds of stories from around the country:

I was on the dance floor when a group of lads started to lift up my skirt and tried to pull down my pants. I just walked away.

I am a beautician and I was in a consulting room with a client. He asked me if I offered extra. I said no, and he exposed himself to me and started to masturbate. I asked him to stop; he said sorry, he couldn't control himself. I was visibly pregnant, yet it didn't stop him. He's been in since as if nothing happened.

I was on the tube this week. A man kept putting his hand on top of mine on the handrail; every time I moved it, he did it again. I stood on tiptoe in order to reach the handle above me. I'm not tall, so it was difficult. He then stood so close behind me that his groin rubbed against me. I couldn't do anything.

I stopped going to clubs because I was fed up of being touched inappropriately by strangers. Now I'm a barmaid, I just have to deal with 'banter' in a work context!

I'm a teacher. Last week in the corridor at school, I overheard a girl tell her boyfriend to wait while she went to the loo. After she walked off, the boy's two mates laughed at him. One said to him, 'Don't let her order you around; keep that bitch on a leash.' They were fourteen.

All the hundreds of stories I have read have one thing in common: the victim never mentioned the abuse to their parents, their partners and most certainly not the police.

Police figures will never show the reality; it is all a part of normal life. Women shrug it off as just one of those things. Having to tell a man that 'No, I don't want to get in your car' is a pain but no biggie. I've met girls who did get in the car. There are vulnerable girls in Rotherham, Rochdale, Oxford and – well, pretty much every town and every city everywhere, and certain men know where to look for them.

Violence against women is everywhere. On every street a woman is taking a beating. Or just keeping quiet waiting for the ordeal to be over. At every nightspot in the country a teenage girl is being groped and shamed. Every school in the country has a kid whose time there is respite from what they see at home. When a problem is everywhere, we need everyone to join in the fight to stop it.

It is a shame that I have to say this, but I'll be accused of being a man hater if I don't. I don't think all men are rapists. I don't think all men are sexist. I don't think all men commit violence against women, or against anyone for that matter. Most men are absolutely smashing. Most men would gladly stand shoulder to shoulder with their sisters and demand better. Unfortunately, the vocal minority too often let them down. Too many men get immediately defensive when women raise this issue. I'm here to say, 'Don't always assume we are talking about you, dude.'

We need every man who sees his mate touching a woman's bottom to speak up. Don't laugh; it's *not* just one of those things. We need every man who hears another man referring to a woman as worthless, a bitch, a whore or a slag to speak up. No one should ever let the statement 'She was asking for it' pass without comment. If men think their mates, their sons, their dads are being a bit leery, they need to tell them to pack it in.

Most of all, when a woman says it happens, don't tell her she's wrong. Don't think it means she thinks all men do it. Don't think it means she thinks you are like them. Just listen!

If every man who was on our side spoke up, it would drown out the very loud minority who don't support women's rights. I know that there are hundreds of noisy men taking to the Internet right now to shout at me and say things like 'She wishes someone wanted to rape her.' Let's not let them be the voice that stands out.

This is not an Us vs Them issue. Women fighting for their right to live free from violence are not attacking men; they are defending women. The more men who join us in the fight, the less it will happen. More women will speak up, more women will be able to go out dancing, settle down with a partner and live full lives free from fear. We must encourage every woman who suffers any sort of violence to report it to the police; I wish I had. All I ask of every man is simple: please just tell us that you believe us. Otherwise we will carry on keeping it secret, taking it as if we deserve it.

When looking at the fight to stop violence against women in the UK, we can see women engaging in protest after protest. Reclaiming the night, laying down red shoes to signify women murdered at the hands of their partners, displaying banners and signs. I know from all my work, and endless academic studies, that tackling women's rights issues here and around the world is always best organised and best realised when women self-advocate. We won't be given a break; we will have to take it for ourselves. If you were going to say anything to support a victim of violence, my advice is simple: the words 'I believe you' are all you really need.

The truth about violence against women is hard to hear. It makes us feel unsafe; it is other, it is not us. The truth is, we won't be safe *until* we face it. If there was ever a thing to speak up about, to use your voice to scream from the rooftops, this is the one.

THE TRUTH ABOUT

SISTERHOOD

Women have a rough deal in society. In the UK, we are still seventy-seven years away from achieving equal pay. We have hardly any of the top jobs and get well chuffed when a woman lands one, so much so that we splash her across all the magazines – check out this lady scientist, or ogle this female CEO. We women are still overwhelmingly the victims of domestic and sexual violence; statistics show that nothing has changed in that area of our lives in the past forty years. So we get beaten, abused and raped more often. It's crap that caring responsibilities still mostly fall to us, and our razors and deodorant cost more because they are pink. But the bonds we are able to form, the friendship and loyalty we can foster with each other is unrivalled among our beardy counterparts. Sisterhood and sorority is the reason I am glad to be a woman.

Much of the debate about why women don't achieve in the world of work and politics revolves around the idea of networks. I sat through hours of discussions and evidence sessions on the gender pay gap while on the Women and Equalities Committee in Parliament. Again and again the issue of networks and networking came up. It seems very strange to me that even in modern-day discussions on women and work the same old tropes about men being on the golf course or in the bars after work crop up. Jeremy Corbyn himself commented that we should ban after-work drinking because it discriminates against women. I might be mistaken, but I live in the twenty-first century, and I'm not sure why everyone thinks that the modern world is like an episode of *The Good Life* (I bagsy being Margo) or *The Fall and Rise of Reginald Perrin*. I've managed to remain gainfully employed and never picked up a golf club, save for when I play crazy golf with my kids, which I don't think counts.

Commentators and politicians alike return time and again to the idea of the old-boy network in trying to understand why that stubborn glass ceiling remains only barely cracked. There is no doubt at all when looking around the green benches in Westminster that there is some truth in a network of Eton boys looking after each other. I was once walking through the lobby with David Cameron and had the briefest of chats with him. What struck me most was the fact that he walked, stood and spoke like a man who had always thought it was inevitable he would end up as prime minister. It was as if he just had to walk through door A, then door B and back through door A and eureka – the top job in the country was his. I suppose that is what you get if you are surrounded by people who seem to achieve everything they set their eyes on. The circles the Camerons move in are, I am sure, considerably different from those I inhabit. I am guessing Mrs Cameron Senior didn't paint little David's face with CND signs and make him stand with a 'Peace and Love' balloon on the steps of Birmingham City Council House. If a five-year-old David Cameron had stood up in a school assembly and exclaimed sweetly, 'When I grow up I want to be prime minister,' people wouldn't just have cooed at the sweet little boy and his funny ideas; they would have started lobbying him about fox hunting.

Around the time he was facing heat for his family's offshore accounts, I wrote an article for the *Huffington Post* about how David Cameron wasn't clever, just privileged. A snippy critic came back at me on Twitter and exclaimed, 'I bet you couldn't have got into the school David Cameron went to.' To which I was able to reply, 'No, I certainly couldn't have, what with having a womb and no money. I couldn't have got into David Cameron's school – a school that didn't make it into the top 100 schools for A-level results this year – but I did go to the school ranked 41st and I didn't pay a bean.' Stick that in your privileged pipe and smoke it.

So I am not denying that these networks exist; I just think we should stop talking them up the way we do. We need to be mindful of highlighting the unfairness but at the same time stop thinking that these are networks we have to be part of to succeed. Sod the Establishment way; let's make our own networks and let's make them the enviable ones.

I wish we gave the same credence to the amazing and strong networks that women build up over their lives. In my view, women's relationships are the building blocks for us to achieve success, and we should try in some way to formalise how we send the ladder down to those who come along behind us in the way that men seem to. I recently attended a meeting in Parliament with ten or so women from the Khyber Pakhtunkhwa Assembly's Women's Provincial Parliamentary Caucus to talk about British politics and the role of women. This group from one of the regional assemblies in Pakistan were all from different political parties. What they had created was a power base to push their individual parties and the assembly itself on issues that mattered to them. I was in awe of their gumption and how far away we are from such a formalised women's lobby in the UK. One of the Conservative government whips – who will remain nameless, but she herself will know who I am talking about – once said to me in a moment of exasperation at the maleness of the UK Parliament, 'I tell you what, Jess, if all the women in this place got together, we'd sort this country out overnight.' Perhaps in the future women in the UK will take a leaf out of the book of the Khyber Pakhtunkhwa Assembly's Women's Provincial Parliamentary Caucus, though I hope we come up with a snappier name.

Women's relationships and friendships are so fierce that I am not sure why we have not been able to achieve more with our collective strength. Shoulder to shoulder into the fray and all that jazz. I think it is perhaps because the idea of 'the sisterhood' has been disputed. For some reason, women run away from the idea that we should stick together. If I were doing a vox pop in the street and I asked women, 'Do you think there is a sisterhood that helped you succeed?' most respondents would be stumped, because we cannot recognise it for what it is. Like so many things that women do, we take it for granted, and don't congratulate ourselves on how we are directly or indirectly helping each other.

While I was writing this book, I put a post on Facebook asking my friends to tell me about the most sisterly things anyone had ever done for them. Here are some of the responses.

I was eleven, fairly new to high school. I broke my right wrist so I couldn't take notes. Jes (who I don't think I'd ever spoken to before that day) said she would take my notes for me. And she did, in every single class for four weeks. We became best friends. We'd talk on the phone for hours. We'd write stupidly long letters to each other (pre email and messenger!). We learned about growing up together (illicit piercings, tattoos and boys), went clubbing together as soon as we were sixteen. Kept in touch when I left school for college and she stayed at sixth form. She died a couple of months after that in a car accident – her first solo journey as a seventeen-year-old. I still miss my 'sister' Jes Smith. (Gemma)

Team of unconnected but bloody marvellous women helped with school runs, took toddler out and brought food when I was really poorly in pregnancy. Also, two lovely female colleagues for taking the rap for an omission of mine with an aggressive boss. And our lovely Jo Cox for sitting down next to me at a male-dominated party conference fringe when I was self-conscious about breastfeeding and feeding her own wee one in solidarity. (Claire)

One who took me in when I was escaping from my first husband, and hid me in her bedroom when he came looking for me, and two who put up with him endlessly turning up on their doorsteps and trying to get them to tell him stuff about me. (Nan)

My friend gave me a bed when I was a victim of domestic violence. She is still my best friend. (Pat)

One of my dear friends, Jess Southwood, told me that I was her example of a sisterly act. Jess wrote:

My ex-husband had sunk into a deep depression following the stillbirth of our daughter and the failure of his business. I was constantly travelling for work; our two living children were little. We were overwhelmed. Jess had come over one Saturday with the boys, as she often did. It was late October and I hadn't been in the garden since summer. Jess popped out for a cigarette – the only person to open the back door in all that time except my husband. She told me that I needed to see the garden. It was full of empty bottles and cans, hidden in the bushes, piled up against the wall, unseen from the house. Mountains of his cigarette butts teetered around the chair where he sat all evening in his coat and gloves. I was in shock. Horribly confronted by his condition and addiction.

Jess got bin bags from under my sink and together we cleared the garden. There were thirty bags of rubbish. When I came to the cigarette butts she said, 'Oh I'll do that, it doesn't bother me; I'm a smoker.' And scooped those stinking piles into bags without a moment of hesitation. She was perfect: no judgement or pity. It was the kindest thing anyone has ever done for me.

The thing about each and every one of these stories, including the one about me, is that if I'd asked the women who did these things, they wouldn't have realised it was a big issue. That's how I feel about Jess's story. I don't think I did anything particularly special; it's what anyone would have done in those circumstances, right? Just like with all the unpaid work we do for free, all the caring, all the extra hours in the office to get the job done expecting no reward.

We have got to get better at recognising the awesomeness and power of our actions. I'm going to start right here, right now. I'm going to sing the praises of all the women without whom I wouldn't be where I am today, and try to show that the sisterhood is an actual thing, and that men should want to have what we have instead of us trying to assimilate with some 1970s golf-club fantasy land.

My mom, Jean, died when I was in my twenties. There is no one, nor will there ever be anyone, who inspires me as much. She was the kindest, bravest and funniest woman alive. The mother of three sons and little me, the youngest of the bunch, we became each other's feminist icons. The daughter of a single mother, living on dinner-lady wages, my mom fought every 1950s path laid out for her. She resisted the job in the haberdashery section at Beatties department store, as was her foretold future, and stuck two fingers up to the teacher who told her she'd never find a man as she couldn't make a jelly. Got herself educated and became pretty eminent. She made pretty damn fine milk-jelly rabbits for me every birthday, as well as keeping a man, and filing reports to improve the NHS.

My mother was definitely not as cocksure as I am, but she wouldn't suffer fools gladly. I remember her running down the road in her battered old towelling coat chasing off a leafleter from the National Front in a rare moment of anger: 'Stick your filth where the sun don't shine, you racist.' Usually, though, she was calmer than me, much shyer and less confrontational. But that didn't make her any less active as a campaigner. In the late seventies, my nan was prescribed a dodgy drug for angina called Eraldin. The side effects were life-changing. The drug dried up Nan's tear glands. She told me once that every time she blinked, it was like having sandpaper rubbed across her eyes. My mom was not going to take this lying down. She worked with a group of other affected families to create a campaign group that successfully sued the drug company for millions of pounds, which was then distributed to thousands of families. I still wear the sapphire and diamond ring that was bequeathed to her as a symbol of gratitude from one of the women she helped.

When I was growing up, there was a big old oak cupboard in our house that we called the Eraldin cupboard. I thought an Eraldin cupboard was something that everyone had, like an airing cupboard. It wasn't until I was much older that I found out it was so called because it was where my mom stored all the papers of the thousands of case studies she had gathered. Not everyone has an Eraldin cupboard, but then not everyone was raised by a woman so willing to stick it to the man.

The women in my family epitomised the idea of a network of support. It might seem a completely feminised sort of networking, but without my nan and my grandma stepping up to look after us when we were kids, my mother would never have got anywhere near the glass ceiling. My mother was not just a great mom, who helped me with my school work and my degree; she was also fierce about getting me work experience and building me up as a woman who could have a career. By the time I was old enough to be applying for jobs, she had a pretty senior role and would make me practise over and over again what I might say in an interview. No job application would ever be submitted without her casting an eye over it and telling me where I was going wrong. She trained me to be a worker, to become indispensable once I'd got my foot in the door, and she taught me how to negotiate for better terms.

The thing that was special about my mom was that she didn't just do this for me. She believed that every kid should have access to the benefits of networks, so she did it for my mates too. Where she could give them work experience she did; she also offered advice and a step up to many of my friends as I was growing up. She took in people who had nowhere else to go and treated them exactly as she treated her own family. She was the greatest supporter of the women who worked with her, and later those who worked for her as she rose up the ranks. No woman would stay my mom's personal assistant for long before she helped them to shimmy up the ladder. When I was eight, I was bridesmaid for my mom's then assistant, Theresa. I'm not sure it's all that common to be a bridesmaid for your mom's staff, but to us, all of these people were family.

My mom was a believer in the power of sharing your networks, and there are lots of women and some men walking around today who can thank her for giving them a chance and then a leg up to something better. Every week young people ring my office and ask for work experience, and because of the way my mom was, I find it impossible to turn them down. It takes quite a lot of juggling (my Westminster office is tiny), but we fit in as many people as possible and we do our very best to find out what each applicant wants out of the experience. Every week, year in, year out, there is someone getting experience in both the London office and my Birmingham office.

When I was elected to Parliament, the first place I visited was the tiny cupboard where Emily Wilding Davidson hid on the night of the census in 1911. This meant that on her census form a woman had a place in Parliament. I love this little cupboard; it epitomises to me how I got to be so privileged as to be able to sit my female derriere on the green benches. In the cupboard is a small plaque in memory of this great and fearless suffragette. When I won my seat, I enthused to my lovely friend Penny about how much I loved the plaque and the cupboard. The following week, she presented me with my very own plaque to put up at Westminster in homage to another feminist who fought for me and women like me to get into this fancy palace. It reads: 'For all the women who roar, especially Jean Trainor.' My mother fought for feminism and equality not for herself but so she could give it away to someone who needed it more.

My parents were always so incredibly proud of how outspoken I was. My dad still is, though he worries about how it can be represented. Just after I was elected, a man with an interest in political archives brought to my constituency office a copy of the minutes from a House of Commons debate from 1977 all about my mom's campaign. The debate was led by Syd Tierney MP, then Member of

Parliament for my family's home in Birmingham Yardley, the area I now represent. My mom would be glad that my bum fills the space where his once sat. She's been gone five years, but her ways, her parenting, still guide every decision I make. Her greatest skill was to love and be loved, fight and win, without anyone realising she had done it.

No one will ever replace my mom, but my mother-in-law, Diana, does a pretty good job. She ran away from home at sixteen because, as the eldest and only girl, her prospects involved little more than being around to look after her brothers. In later life she wears this job well, as now nearly every day she takes part in raising my kids. My heart breaks a tiny bit when they accidentally call me Nan, because some weeks she sees them more than I do. I comfort myself with the fact that it's better to have too many people *in loco parentis* than too few. Two kick-ass women raising your boys is better than one. I don't call her Mom, but that's what she is to me.

Diana is a painful overachiever at most things: baking, sewing, knitting, gardening, crafting, photography and beekeeping. She often makes cakes or toys for me to present at community events and school fetes as if I had made them myself; a bit like Cyrano de Bergerac but with flour, eggs and sticky-back plastic. I can never pass them off as my own for very long, mainly because some of the things are so good, no one would ever believe I had the time or the necessary skills to make them. She does all this for me not only because she wants to see and raise her grandchildren, but also because she wants me to succeed in achieving my ambitions. She wants to live in a world where it is possible for a young woman with children to be an MP, because she grew up in a world where it wasn't. She threatened to get a T-shirt that said, 'Check me out, my daughter-in-law is an MP'. Any success is ours, not mine. Without Diana, I would never be in Parliament.

I don't have any actual sisters, but I've had a wide range of sisters-in-law and 'outlaws', as my mom and dad used to call their children's unmarried partners. When you have three brothers, at times it can seem like they are courting a conveyor belt of women. Some of these women didn't just go out with one brother; after all, why settle for one when there are spares? One of the most memorable outlaws was a woman called Paula, who had a thick Yorkshire accent and a crystal ball. She used to say things like 'I don't have a middle name but I know it's Mary.' I think her defining moment was when she stood drunk and swaying on the kitchen table in my parents' home at my grandad's wake and sang 'Que Sera, Sera'. The only person more exuberant than her in my family, who would have appreciated the drunken exhibitionism of a beautiful woman, was sadly safely in his coffin. I suppose it was a fitting if not wholly appropriate tribute.

With the exception of only a few, I am still in touch with these in-laws and outlaws. I've attended their weddings to more suitable partners and cooed over their babies. The sisters-in-law who stuck are in many ways closer to me than my brothers are; they are the people I arrange things with, talk to about caring duties, go on nights out with. I imagine it is like having sisters except we don't squabble, and they are less willing to join in with the gentle ribbing of the rest of my family than they would if they were blood.

I'm not a naturally girlie girl. Being the youngest of four kids, with no sisters, meant I wore boys' clothes – mainly seventies brown and orange striped jumpers with 'Champ' written across the front. By the time they got to me, they were misshapen from a decade of wear. My mom hadn't ever had to plait or even comb hair until I came along, so until I was about ten, I either had a boy's bowl cut or a very, very tangled mane. Never once was I dressed in pretty frocks with beautifully ribboned French plaits, though occasionally Ceri Morgan, who lived down the road, would bring around a big black bin bag of hand-me-down clothes. I grew up surrounded by boys, most of my mates were boys, and really I wanted to be a boy. Even now I don't know what all those potions are that my friends seem to take on holiday with them. I don't moisturise my skin, I don't polish my nails and I can't do anything with my hair other than brush it, which if I'm honest doesn't happen every day.

My first ever proper female friend was Bryony, who lived four doors down from us. She was my window into a girlie world. She owned scrunchies (an accessory that appears – inexplicably – to be back), she used to paint her nails and she made earrings and brooches out of Fimo. She had a dressing table in her room – as far as I was concerned, something only to be found in Disney princess stories – and posters on her wall of New Kids on the Block and Kylie Minogue. In my house, there was no room for brightly coloured pop memorabilia. My brothers adorned the walls with dark twisty rock posters and psychedelic funk depictions; liking pop music was simply not an option. Had I put up a poster of the pint-sized Australian pop princess, it would not have been long before it was adorned with a Hitler moustache at the very least, and my beloved father's left-wing stance meant I wasn't allowed to watch American TV or Australian soaps anyway. For me, the 1980s was seen through a prism of teenage boys and the miners' strike.

Bryony's house was the place to watch *Neighbours* and Disney films (my father used to bark that Disney was a fascist) and read *Smash Hits* or *Just Seventeen*. Bryony and I were inseparable, and to this day we are still incredibly close. Together we learnt about the incredible bond of female friendship, and as we have grown up, this has meant sharing any power and influence we have to try and improve the position of the other. When I first considered standing as an elected representative, Bryony was out there campaigning in the cold, and was pictured with her kids on my leaflets. When Bryony was hideously discriminated against by her employer because of pregnancy and maternity leave, it was my house where she came to drink wine and draft her letter of complaint. When she started an online kids' clothes company, I made sure I was a patron and that everyone I knew was one too.

I now have an amazing group of life-enriching women friends. My mates are wet-your-knickers hilarious. I wish I could have a wedding every year just so there was a chance to dress up and make lavish speeches about each and every one of them. These women have sat in A&E waiting rooms with me all night, kept me laughing by allowing me to update their online dating profiles while my mom was in surgery in another country and I was too pregnant to travel. They picked my kids up because I missed my train, forgot about a meeting or was in labour, and they left casseroles on my doorstep every day for the two weeks after my mom died.

We have an unwritten rota for taking care of each other. A simple text of a joke that has been running for over ten years lifts the dullest day. A bunch of flowers when someone gets a promotion, paying for a massage when you know they are stressed, even though they didn't tell you. More than anything, it is the laughing we do together; it is infectious, it hurts. Sometimes we laugh until we can hardly breathe. It takes work to be a good friend; it's not just being the life and soul of the party. It takes effort to buy gifts, remember birthdays or anniversaries that are happy or sad. It means looking after your mates' kids and feeding their cats, not just expecting them to do it for you. I think friendships take the same amount of work as successful romantic relationships.

When one of us does well, it feels like we've all had a win. When I was selected to be the Labour candidate for Birmingham Yardley, I had a full-time job, I was a local councillor and I had two small kids. It was inevitable in this situation that something had to give, and my social life was the thing I had to sacrifice. My girlfriends never faltered, though. They learnt to accept that I would always be late, or if they wanted to see me, that meant coming to a Labour Party fund-raiser. They book holidays and never expect me to lift a finger in organising things; they just tell me the dates and sort it out for me. Don't get me wrong, they are not perfect, and I am sure they take the piss and get annoyed with me behind my back, but they have the good nature to keep it from me. On one occasion I was really late to dinner at one of their homes. By the time I arrived, all the food had gone and I was left with nothing but a bag of Doritos. This has become a long-standing joke: when anyone cooks, someone brings a bag of Doritos for me to eat when I finally arrive. If they are reading this, I don't like the flaming-hot ones; I'm all about the tangy cheese.

I could not do my job without my mates. It's not just all the favours they do for me, but the fact that when things are hideous and scary – and that happens quite a lot in my job – nothing makes me feel better than sitting around laughing with them. They keep me grounded and in touch with the real world. In Westminster I get to do cool things and meet famous people. My mate Jess has instigated a rule for any night out, where I am only allowed to say five fancy things and after that she raps my knuckles each time. They take me away from visions of battered women, bombs in Syria and online vitriol. They are incredibly proud of me, and celebrate my achievements, but they are not overly interested in my political life or what telly programme I have been on; they just want to drink Prosecco and dance to nineties RnB.

Westminster is a tough gig. Politics is naturally competitive. The corridors of the Commons are lined with 'look at me' wallpaper and carpeted with jealousy. Not if you are a Labour woman, however. If you are a Labour woman, you join the 'you bloody well better be as good as you can be' sorority. Within weeks of my arrival in Westminster, many of my fellow female MPs had sat me down over a cuppa and told me how they would help me be marvellous. The women in the Parliamentary Labour Party cheer when another speaks. When I fall over or stand strong, supportive text messages flood in. Of course there are exceptions, but the sisterhood in Parliament exists. I cannot think of a single problem I might face in my personal or political life that I couldn't find a member of the Women's PLP to help me with. Most of the women in the PLP consider that the advancement of women in the Commons and in the country is an intrinsic part of the job description. We are not just constituency representatives and Westminster legislators, we are also feminist activists.

The sisterhood in Parliament means added unpaid work for the women there. When we make demands about gender balance on committees and boards, we all have to step up to fill the seats. Remember that there are fewer of us, so when we fight to keep up with men's voices in Parliament, we all have to do extra. I am on two parliamentary committees, I chair or co-chair (with another woman) three All-Party Parliamentary Groups, and I am the chair of the Women's PLP. It is fairly rare to be on two select committees, but if I hadn't done it, one of them wouldn't have had a woman on it at all. It's also worth pointing out that women are more likely to hold marginal seats, which need more attention, and Labour women are more likely to hold seats in urban communities, with the huge amount of casework that comes with representing areas of multiple deprivation. No extra income or resources are garnered from taking on extra parliamentary responsibilities, or having huge, complex caseloads. So the female MPs in the PLP really do rely on each other for support.

When I first arrived in Westminster, there was one woman who really stood out in terms of offering support and sorority. Jo Cox is gone now, and I miss her every time I sit down on those green benches. Her family asked if people could bring a simple page of A4 paper to her funeral detailing our memories of her. The pages were to be turned into a memory book for Cuillin and Leyla, her beautiful children, so that as they grow up, they can dip into it and be surrounded by the love other people feel for them and their mum. This was my offering.

Dear Cuillin and Leyla,

'What's our plan?' were the words your mum said to me as she served me lasagne on your lovely houseboat. She had just put you two to bed, but you sneaked out to say hello to me, just like my children do.

'*The boys all have grand plans, we've got to stick together.*'

Your mum and I were determined not to let our political lives be sidelined by the fact that we were women. The way we decided we would fight for what mattered to us was by sticking together, supporting each other.

It may not seem like the most coherent plan, but in politics in Westminster love and loyalty is rare. Its power therefore is huge.

Your mum's friendship to me meant that I could be brave. There were many times when she or I were going to say something or write something that would mean meanies would come out of the woodwork and shout at us or call us names. We would give each other a call or a text to say what we were going to do. I suppose it was a bit like a bat signal in Batman, *so that the other would know to bring backup. We would defend each other publicly. Praise each other whenever we did something and check in with each other when the meanies were getting loud, to give love and kisses. As you grow up, you will watch her speeches in the Commons. I was lucky enough to see them live. She would always text me before she spoke and I would with her, and whenever we could we would make sure the other was there.*

Love is how I will remember your mum. We walked shoulder to shoulder into the fray.

All my love,

Jess P x

Jo was sisterhood personified. She did not wait for bonds to be built naturally; she made them happen and she worked hard to maintain them. A woman with two children under six and a difficult job challenged the Syrian government, took her fight for refugees to the Russian ambassador, led the charge for humanitarian support around the world and set up and sat on new committees to do this. She represented a mixed constituency with real needs and tough battles but still found time for the hard work of being a supportive friend.

There is a definite sisterhood in Parliament. It stretches across party lines and includes not just MPs but also the female lobby journalists sent to watch us all. Recently the well-respected journalist Isabel Hardman was referred to as 'totty' by an old-guard Tory chap named Colonel Bob Stewart. Isabel is the deputy editor of the *Spectator*. She is not totty; she is a woman doing her job. When she tweeted about the incident, she found herself in the middle of a political story. Female journalists from different schools of thought came out to either defend her assertions of sexism or tell her to 'suck it up and be flattered'. I remember having a chat with one Tory woman about the incident before the identity of Colonel Bob had been released and she said, 'Sounds to me like he deserves a sharp kick in the balls.' The vast majority of women in Parliament came out in support of Isabel.

I have felt immense sorority from some of the Tory and SNP women in Parliament. On one occasion, after I was involved in a heated argument with a Tory parliamentary private secretary across the chamber of the Commons, Therese Coffey, then the Deputy Leader of the House, pretty much sent him off with a flea in his ear, demanding he apologise and buy me a gin and tonic to boot. I also received an apology from the departmental whip. Therese stuck up for me not because she thought I was weak but because she recognises that senior Tory men having a pop at new female MPs is probably pretty discouraging. Even though we are on different sides, she wants to encourage women's voices.

Having said all these lovely and tear-jerking things about sisterhood and how marvellous it is, there is plenty of evidence to disprove my assertions. There are many women – in Parliament and elsewhere – who infantilise their male colleagues, who feel that we have to put a spoonful of sugar in for the men, as if we should always be apologising to them for where women are now. I have seen this time and time again with women in politics. In nearly every discussion I have with Tory MPs about feminist issues, there is, without fail, always a voice that pipes up and says, 'We must consider how this is going to look to the men. We don't want to isolate them or make them feel like we are attacking them.'

It may come as a shock to readers to find that Parliament is in no way family-friendly and does little to help women progress. Shocker! Timings, procedures and long-held practices are incredibly inflexible and make being a parent and an MP really unappealing. At usually no more than a day's notice, sometimes just an hour's notice, you can be called to stay in the House until 3 a.m. Imagine if you were a nursing mother, or providing care for a dying parent. We can all dance around and pretend that the men in Parliament are bearing these responsibilities as much as their female counterparts, but that simply is not true. Of course there are some notable examples of men walking the halls of Westminster with their babies in tow. Karl Turner, an MP in Hull, is such a doting father, I think he brings his baby daughter to work even when he doesn't have to. Johnny Reynolds' kids can usually be found eating lunch in one of Westminster's canteens, always providing entertainment and bags of cheek to boot. These examples stand out because they are rare. Many women in Parliament, myself included, have to make apologetic phone calls to our children week in, week out, to tell them that once again we will not be home when we thought we would.

Recently a cross-party group of women in the Commons called for a meeting with the Speaker of the House to discuss the issue of modernising Parliament. Among the many things that were talked about was the subject of improving the ratio of women's voices in the Commons. There is nothing written down about what order speakers are called in the chamber during a debate; however, there are a number of conventions that are followed for who gets picked first. It is fairly complicated to explain, but if there is a debate on a popular subject and lots of people ask to speak, a time limit is usually imposed. Depending on how many people want to speak, this usually settles at around five minutes to start and then reduces as the debate goes on. I once crammed what should have been a ten-minute speech on tax credit reductions into two minutes. However, the time limit is usually put in place after the first few speakers have spoken, meaning that those who get in first have more air time.

The unwritten rules about who gets called first in a debate are loosely based on seniority (how long you have been in the Commons). This naturally favours older male speakers who have been in the Commons for years; it will take another few decades before we have anywhere near as many senior women as we have senior men. The longest-serving MP in the Commons is known as the Father of the House; once again, you might be shocked to hear that there has never been a Mother of the House. The second category of parliamentarians who get priority in debates is chairs of select committees. This again naturally favours men: of the twenty-seven select committees in the UK Parliament, only seven are chaired by women.

During a debate, an MP from the government (currently Conservative) benches is invited to speak first, followed by one from a pool of all of the parties on the opposition benches. Given that there are only 68 women out of a total of 329 Tory MPs, their increased speaker ratio again marginalises women's voices. To put it simply: if you are a woman, especially one on the opposition benches, you could spend all day trying to speak in a debate and never get called before time runs out. Even if you do eventually get called to speak, by the time it's your turn, the time limit has reduced to about three minutes for you to make your points, while the senior men were allowed to orate for around twenty minutes no matter whether they had anything to say. Parliament's unwritten rules and procedures mean that men's voices have the advantage. (I must say that the current Speaker John Bercow is a fair and even-handed man who wants the Commons to modernise, but the battle is not his alone.)

The group of women assembled began to explain all this to the Speaker, and ask that as well as adjusting some of the seniority protocols, there might be some nod towards an unwritten rule on gender balance as well. We were not demanding that every other speaker was a woman, just some understanding and action on the obvious unfairness. Sat next to me was a relatively young new Tory MP (who would benefit from said arrangement). She piped up that she didn't think it right that women be given 'special treatment'. Special treatment! Special frickin' treatment! Er, I think the special treatment has been given to the men in Parliament, you know, the ones I just described who have all the advantages and are able to pretty much do and say what they want when they want because they were elected at a time when women in Parliament was just a precious little idea. Some of these men have been saying their bit since before I was born; some of them think we women have too much to say for ourselves; some of them have probably stood on their feet in the House of Commons for more minutes than I have been alive. We were not asking for special treatment that might upset the men, as if they are dainty little flowers who cannot face the fact that they might have to wait until a woman has spoken. We were asking for fair treatment and that some ancient established hierarchical protocol could be stretched to, you know, include half the population.

Said Tory MP, in her clipped, could-be-from-literally-anywhere posh accent, declared that we must be careful of the feelings of our male counterparts and mustn't appear difficult. To which I exclaimed, 'Bab, I don't give a toss if people think I am being difficult. Where's your sisterhood?'

Because female Conservative Party members have been more successful, i.e. they have been responsible for the two female prime ministers we've had, I don't think they recognise all that has been done by difficult bloody women to make that possible. On International Women's Day in 2016, many women and some of the men in Parliament gathered in the Commons chamber for a debate about the event. It was an opportunity for parliamentarians to celebrate women's voices and achievements and speak up about the many issues facing women around the world. The Tory front bench quickly filled with female ministers, an array of colour in a usually drab grey line-up. They looked pleased as Punch as they sat together. Harriet Harman, who was sitting next to me, glanced across to the gathered women and said audibly,

'You're very welcome.' The moment of slight snark alluded to the fact that Harriet and others like her have spent thirty-odd years in this ancient place trying to make it slightly less ancient. The women who have benefited should be willing to be difficult too.

Conservative women might not realise it, but it was the goddam sisterhood that delivered the possibility of having a female prime minister in the first place. It is such a shame that so many of them seem to have pulled up the drawbridge rather than continuing to fight for their sisters, in the Commons and the country. I think things are changing, but you will still find few Tory women who proudly call themselves feminists, opting instead for the men-appeasing statement: 'I think of myself as more of an equalist.' Every time I hear it, I want to throw up a bit of sick in my mouth and scream in their faces, 'Darling, you wouldn't even have a vote in this place, let alone your bum on a seat here, if it weren't for the feminist women who were willing to die for you. Show some respect.'

Many Tory women have turned right, into a cul-de-sac where their sex continue to be second-class citizens. They seem unwilling to speak truth to power on gender and instead prefer words of appeasement. Margaret Thatcher didn't do anything for women, in the UK or around the world. She didn't speak out and promote women or equality. Perhaps Theresa May will be better; perhaps her government's policies won't have a disproportionately negative effect on women – poor women to boot. Perhaps she will say 'sod it' to the men in her party and follow up with 'I'm a goddam feminist and the big momma of this country and I'm gonna goddam well look after my sisters and make sure we strive for them to have everything you have ever had.' Don't bank on it. I imagine she will say, 'Never mind the decades of women who fought so that I could have this privilege, I'm all right, Jack.' Because saying 'I'm all right, Jill' would just be political correctness gone mad.

Difficult women change the world but so rarely reap the rewards. As I watched Hillary Rodham Clinton's concession speech in November, the anger, shock and disbelief I had felt since Trump was announced as the 45th President of the United States slipped away and turned to deep, painful sorrow. I wept breathless sobs and felt the heat of burning tears on my face when she said, 'To all the women, especially the young women who put their faith in this campaign and in me, I want you to know that nothing has made me prouder than to be your champion.' I would not have supported Hillary just because she was a woman. I supported her because for decades she has campaigned for the rights of women. Her politics don't necessarily align with mine and I think she has made some mistakes. But, my god, I felt she was my champion. I've never felt that about Theresa May, Margaret Thatcher or Sarah Palin. Hillary was said to be the establishment patsy but the truth is, had she been a Republican woman, she, like Tory women in the UK, would certainly have had an easier path to victory.

Difficult women – or dangerous women, as we get called – have more anti-establishment credentials in one line of their beautiful lived-in faces than Trump has in his whole ugly orange body. Clinton finished her speech by saying, 'To all the little girls watching this, never doubt that you are valuable and powerful and deserving of every chance.' Clinton stood for all those little girls. I'm buggered if I'm going to tell anyone that they should try to be the most approachable version of themselves in order to have power. After all, the boys don't have to appease us – they can talk about grabbing a woman's pussy and still get elected.

Now I am going to add a disclaimer paragraph, to stop thousands of angry people writing to me. Men help women progress too, and of course women help men progress. Without my husband and my father, and in fact a man in the regional office of the Labour Party who has always pushed and supported me, I wouldn't have made it. Equally I have sent the ladder down to many young men in my professional life and helped them achieve their political ambitions. The idea of sisterhood is completely misunderstood if it is taken to mean an exclusive club where women will only help women. That's not what it is, that's not what it does. We leave that kind of horrific exclusivity to the Masons, or the gentlemen's clubs of this country. Men are helping men do better everywhere in the world without being forced to write this ridiculous disclaimer. Stick that in your equalist pipe and smoke it.

In the words of the first female US Secretary of State, Madeleine Albright, 'There's a special place in Hell for women who don't help each other!' I believe in the sisterhood. I believe that we shouldn't passively sit back and be glad when women make it, or feel sad when they don't. I think that we should each do our bit to encourage and support women in society. In case you hadn't noticed, we are already doing it. Every single woman in the world when asked could give an example of amazing things another woman has done for her that the other woman would shrug off as if it were nothing. We must be much less squeamish and apologetic about formalising and organising this support, in our workplaces, at our kids' schools, in our families.

When women working at the White House found that they were struggling to make their voices heard, the female staffers in Obama's team used a strategy called 'amplification'. Whenever a woman made a key point, other women would repeat it, giving credit to its author. This forced the men in the room to recognise the contribution. Lyn Brown, a Labour MP, told me that women in the Labour Party used to do the same but called it 'sharing the broken record'. If I was in a meeting where someone took credit for a woman's idea without acknowledging her, I would definitely pipe up with 'Yeah, Dave, we heard that already, when Lyn said it.' If someone did it to me, I would say, 'Er, didn't I just say that?' I get that everyone is not as bold as me, so we've got to stick up for each other. We must promote other women when they do well and be their cheer squad. This is not because we are precious princesses who cannot speak for ourselves; it is because men are doing enough back-slapping of each other, and we should do it too.

Sisterhood is not about blindly supporting any woman, or picking a woman over a man even if a man is better. It is just about recognising all the amazing stuff that women do for each other and putting a little bit of effort into paying that forward. I've found in my life that women sticking together only offends people who love to shriek 'Meritocracy!' as if they are playing blinkered bingo. Sisterhood should be promoted and encouraged. We should ignore the naysayers who only don't like it because it means sharing a bit of their privilege. Funny, that.

THE TRUTH ABOUT
WINNING ELECTIONS

The elation I felt at winning my seat in the 2015 general election is very clear when watching the video of my victory. Bear in mind that it was 6 a.m. and I had been awake for at least twenty-four hours. I'd done nothing but eat crisps and drink coffee all day. I was wired. As the amount of votes I received was read out, I bent double, hanging my head and my hair to the floor like a rag doll. As I reappear to the crowd, I am laughing raucously.

The returning officer continued to read out the results after mine. It's a bit like a wedding, where you hear people's full names for the first time and have a bit of a chuckle at them: 'Jonathan Alexander Marvin Hemming'. They are invariably not the names you have called them for the previous few months of bitter campaigning. I can't remember if I was particularly aware of it at the time, but when I looked again at the footage, it hit me. In the line-up of dutiful-looking candidates, I am a shock of colour in bright emerald green with a huge necklace bought for a fiver in the Topshop sale that I felt at the time was reminiscent of something Daenerys Targaryen, Mother of Dragons, would wear. I stand out in the row of suits, proudly beaming, the only woman on the ballot.

As the names of the minority parties and their handfuls of votes were being read out, I had a moment of panic: was I supposed to go along the row and speak to each person? Or was I supposed to just skate past them all rudely? I hadn't been trained how to commiserate with my opponents, some of whom I utterly detested and some I really liked. As I was called to the stage to make my victory speech, I look a bit like a kid at a prize-giving, slightly bewildered. My shoulders are raised as if I am walking on glass, waiting for a crack to appear. I seem childlike.

I shook the hand of the UKIP chap standing next to me, who was actually really gracious and congratulatory. I had never come across him in the campaign; you don't really need to campaign locally if you have a personality like Farage on the telly to do it for you. Next I came to the previous MP, John Hemming. He was reasonably gracious at first, congratulating me, but it didn't last long before his paternalistic streak showed itself. As I was shaking his hand, he started to tell me what to do, as if he was the big man in the know and I was some feeble pretender. He said, 'You must remember to thank the returning officer,' or something along those lines. On the video on Sky News, all that is audible of this, the briefest of exchanges, is me saying loudly, 'I know what to do, thanks,' in the best Birmingham accent and the attitude of a victorious broad who just beat him in the competition of his life. He was talking to me – the winner, the woman who'd just beaten him – as if I was some silly little girl. At this moment, my whole demeanour changes: I pull my shoulders back and fill with confidence. I am not some silly girl; I am a woman who is about to make a victory speech while a group of men stand and listen.

This is what I said:

Thank you to the returning officer and the brilliant staff here in Birmingham who have done the election so well. I am so thankful to the people of Yardley for putting their trust in me. I will never take it for granted. I will work every single day to keep it.

I do not stand here alone. I must say a huge thank you to the hundreds of people who stood shoulder to shoulder with me throughout this campaign. Thank you to every person who knocked on a door in the rain. Thank you to every person who spent hours talking to people on the phone and took on the letter boxes and the dogs of Yardley. YOU – ARE – AWESOME! With some special mentions to Keith, to Caroline, to the Birmingham Labour Students, to Sara Ward, and of course to Matthew Lloyd for keeping me sane and sticking with me.

I was taught to fight for justice by my mother and father. My mom was the daughter of a dinner lady from Yardley who was given a grant by the Yardley

Great Trust charity to keep poor kids in education in the sixties. She is no longer with me, but she taught me to always speak up for those who have less than you have, to always fight to give a voice to the voiceless and to strive for every child as you would strive for your own children. And so I will.

Every step of this campaign was worth fighting. For every bedroom tax victim, for every nurse left demoralised, for every police officer retired off and women's refuge put at risk. That was what kept us knocking in the rain; we knew it was a fight worth having even when it hurt.

I am very proud to have been elected the Labour Member of Parliament for Yardley. I know that the Labour Party is about everybody and not just the privileged few. I know that we are all better off when we are all better off. Thank you.

I have watched the footage of others on the same night and realise now that their scripts were more subdued, more professional. I've yet to find another example of the victorious candidate literally bending over double and then jumping for joy. Start as you mean to go on.

I get asked all the time what made me want to become an MP. I don't believe in fate or destiny, but looking back, it is a wonder it took me so long to realise I might give it a go. Speaking up on politics was not just encouraged in my family; it was mandatory. If you couldn't talk about politics, you would rarely have been able to join in with conversations at dinner. My dad is a hard-line socialist and my grandad was further to the left still. As a younger man, he had been a commercial artist for a big manufacturing company based in the Midlands. In retirement he had turned his craft to political cartooning, a skill he would lend to only the purist left-wingers in the Labour Party. I used to be forced to spend what felt like hours posing so he could get the image of Maggie Thatcher holding a nuclear missile or Ronald Reagan toting a gun just right. I spent my childhood in the garage churning out leaflets on an old Gestetner-style duplicator. We were a fully operational Labour Party poster production machine: one would paste the board, then pass it to the next sibling to mount the poster, on to me to punch the holes and then to the final brother to thread the string. My dad would then shimmy up thousands of local lamp posts, obscuring the Tory efforts in the process. We were literal standard-bearers for the left.

But I don't usually go into all that; instead I have a series of stock answers, depending on my mood. The joke answer is that I was playing the long game of getting on *Strictly Come Dancing*. Labour women – and men, for that matter – have been overlooked at the Tower Ballroom in Blackpool. I simply couldn't let Ann Widdecombe and Edwina Currie be the face of politics in Lycra and sequins. The workers need representing after all. Alas, Ed Balls, ex-Shadow Chancellor, has since beaten me to this privilege, so now I'll just have to be the first Labour woman to trip the light fantastic.

Another slightly jokey answer, which has some basis in truth, is that I did it as a bet. Wendy, my colleague at Women's Aid, had attended local hustings during the 2010 general election. She returned to our office the next day deflated by the feeling that any of us could have done better, 'They were all useless and uninspiring' was her verdict. Wendy is not a woman with particular party political affiliations, and at the time I myself was not a member of the Labour Party, having stropped off during the Iraq War episode. We sat in our office and decided to have a bet who could become an MP first. I am naturally competitive; as it turned out, Wendy put in no effort whatsoever. She did make a life-size cardboard cut-out of me with my fist in the air, 'power to the people' style, when I was selected, but otherwise she did not keep up her end.

Jokes aside, my inspiration for deciding to run was the coalition government. When the Conservatives won in 2010, I was working at Women's Aid with people at the harsh end of life. I remembered the fights of my youth against Conservative governments. I wanted to do something to fight back again. Like everyone, I used to watch *Question Time* and listen to the soundbites of the government ministers on the news. I felt constantly that the people presented to me knew absolutely bugger all about the things they were talking about. I noticed when they made glaring mistakes and seemed to wilfully misunderstand issues that seemed so very obvious to me. I started to dare to believe that if they could do it, then so could I.

The government's mask well and truly slipped for me at an event I was called to attend organised by the Ministry of Justice. At the time, I was heavily involved in developing services for female offenders in the West Midlands. According to the still brilliant and relevant Corston Report (Baroness Corston is a kick-ass Labour woman), titled *A review of women with particular vulnerabilities in the criminal justice system*, the majority of women in prison have suffered physical, emotional or sexual abuse. For many years it has been the common and correct view that sending women to prison for petty crimes is damaging and costly for them and for society. Centres were set up all over the country to offer community sentences and recovery services for very vulnerable women. The centres were operated in partnership with the probation service and local charities, and they were and still are amazingly successful. If you compare the reoffending rates of women who serve their sentences in a women's centre and those who go to prison, you would be a fool to ever bet on the prison system. The centres also had much better success rates at rehabilitating offenders when they left prison: so-called 'through the gate' services, which allow charities like mine to work with women before and after release.

As part of its flagship justice policy, Transforming Rehabilitation, the coalition government decided that it wanted to privatise the UK Probation Service. The service was not perfect, but privatising it was simply trying to answer a question nobody was asking. The UK was broken up into package areas, and companies were invited to bid for the contracts in different regions. So one company would have the contract for working with offenders in the North East, while a completely different company would hold it in the West Midlands. The contract was going to be 'payment by results', which basically meant that if you were working with an offender who then reoffended, you would lose a percentage of the contract fee.

Because I ran a women's centre, I was called along to a 'stakeholder forum' by the Ministry of Justice. These events are largely a tick-box exercise so that government ministers can pretend they have spoken to the experts. Even if they completely ignore everything that is said to them, they can spin it as if they are listening. In my experience they were not listening. I sat at a table with other providers from around the country; each table was facilitated by a Ministry of Justice civil servant. On our table we talked about how the new private services would work with offenders when they were released from prison. I asked a very simple question about what would happen if one company had done the through-the-gate services and then the prisoner on release had moved hundreds of miles away to a different contract area and accessed a different company's services. In that example, I wanted to know which company would get the payment-by-results funding.

This should not have been a difficult question to answer. To anyone who has ever worked with offenders, it is a basic fact that people do not go to prison anywhere near their homes. They are generally incarcerated hundreds of miles away from where they live. Female prisoners even more so, as there are far fewer women's prisons. You might have noticed as a normal human that there are not prisons in every town. Local prisons for local people is not a thing. I would have thought that the Ministry of Justice might have known this; you know, what with them being in charge of the prisons and all. The civil servant on my table looked at me blankly and said, 'Can't they just stay near the prison and keep working with the first company?' No, my dear fellow, they can't, because they probably have nowhere to live in that area, they have no family in that area, they have never lived there before. Going to prison is not like moving to a new town for a new job and trying to make a go of it. In that moment, I realised that Chris Grayling, the then Secretary of State for Justice (or Lord Chancellor if you want to be fancy), had set about implementing a policy when it was very clear he knew absolutely sod all about how the outside world – let alone his department – actually worked.

In that moment of sad, lamentable desperation about how utterly clueless some politicians are, I thought, I reckon I can do a better job of this. Terrible and wasteful decisions were being made every day by people who had no idea what it was like to run services or deal with people's complex lives. I dared to think I knew better.

So here is the drum-roll moment. The absolute crux of why I stepped on to the platform to become a person who had a voice. The real truth of why I became an MP is because I thought I would be good at it. It really is as simple as that. I thought, and still do think, that I have something to offer. Arrogant, perhaps, even delusional, to think I could do it. I use the term 'delusional' not as a negative in this context; to be able to visualise yourself in a position you deem to be above you might well be delusional, but if you can't think it about yourself, no one else will. A little bit of delusion goes a long way.

I suppose this is my *Lean In* moment, but I want to say in no uncertain terms to people reading this: you are better than you think. Ordinary, everyday people should be much more delusional than they are. When Wendy walked back into our offices after watching the local candidates disappoint her and realised then that the fancy people in suits spouting the scripted lines were not that impressive at all, she was right.

I've talked a bit about how women are much less likely to see themselves in positions of power, or how a man will apply for a job if he meets half the criteria when a woman will not apply because she only fits 90 per cent of it. (And if you want lots more about this, read Cheryl Sandberg's book.) Every day I meet women who say, 'I could never do what you did.' Or 'How on earth did you cope with everything in your life?' Women everywhere are convincing themselves that they don't have the right to be in their positions, or the right to get into positions. Impostor syndrome afflicts each and every one of us. I'd ask everyone who thinks they will look a fool if they speak up in a meeting to remember all the times they encountered someone who was not at all brilliant or amazing but seemed to have a really good job. Chris Grayling is my touchstone, but you could choose any one of those idiots who go on *The Apprentice* and talk a good game but when it comes to it can't even make a sandwich. God only knows why we all walk around thinking everyone else is an absolute master at their job. Every time I read a conspiracy theory about how people in Parliament have masterminded some great cover-up, all I can think is that you have really, *really* overestimated our abilities. I only wish I *was* a member of some crazy Illuminati who can fake the moon landings or such like. In reality, I can barely muster the authority to get Birmingham City Council to install a long-overdue dropped kerb.

I don't want to underplay my achievements, however. Running a campaign to become an MP, holding down a job, being a councillor and being a mom all at the same time was punishing. There were many times I wanted to stop. I did this for two years, most days checking the polls for the likelihood of it all paying off. There were days when Lord Ashcroft and his polling told me I should quit, that I wouldn't win. There is a thing in politics that we call 'candidate's syndrome', which manifests itself as complete and utter despair even if all the evidence in front of you is positive. Every poll might say you will win the election, every person who's door you knock on cheers when they see your face, but you still lie awake at night visualising yourself conceding victory at the count.

I used to practise the speech I would give to my supporters when (not if) we lost, over and over again in my head. It went like this: 'We did all we could, we definitely fought the best fight, I am sorry that it wasn't enough to quite get us over the line ... blah blah blah ... negative platitude after negative platitude. I thought I could win; I just never allowed myself to believe I would.

There were times during the campaign when I really wanted to throw the towel in, to go back to being a normal woman who ate dinner with her family in the evenings and took her children to the park at the weekend. Those were the days when I would have to face hateful accusations from my opponents. I was up against the Liberal Democrat incumbent MP John Hemming. If you Google his name, it won't take you too long to find newspaper articles about his colourful life of multiple mistresses and nominating himself for the *News of the World*'s Love Rat of the Year award. As you do. This was not a man who had shown himself to be favourable to feminists. The frequently told story of his wife catnapping his girlfriend's kitten and being charged in court for the offence gives you an idea of what he drove some of the women in his life to do.

I did not like this man; I still don't. It is safe to say that the feeling was mutual. However, I never used his personal life in my campaign. Pretty much everyone knew about it anyway, and I don't believe that all is fair in love and war. I think that unless your private life affects your job or makes you unsafe, it is not a matter for political campaigns. Also, he had a shocking record while his party was in government, so I didn't need to sink below my principles. His voting record was damning enough. My brother devised a list of insinuating cat puns for me as a joke before one of our hustings debates – whisker away, cat's out of the bag, paws for thought, and many more. Obviously I didn't use them. It turns out the strength of my arguments was good enough.

I would be lying if I said that some of his attacks on me didn't hurt. I acted all tough at the time and brushed things off in public, but fighting political campaigns can be incredibly bruising. Politics is rough and tumble, and I'm far more used to it now than I was then. When you are a candidate, you are haemorrhaging money and time ploughing your life into a campaign. I can't stress enough how much of a risk you have to take to stand. People think we get paid for it. We don't. People think we do it as a full-time job. We don't. Well, we certainly don't unless we are very rich. When you are a candidate fighting against an incumbent MP, you are essentially taking a jelly to a knife fight. You are up against someone whose whole job it is to campaign and work locally, while you are trying to hold down your own job and, in many cases, look after your children. I always felt that the risk I was taking was a potentially selfish one. It was my name splashed across the posters. It was me who was the brand. The risk of us losing was all on my shoulders. I had to work part-time, thus losing some of my family's income, and spend lots of my own money, which I didn't have, trying to make things happen. My husband, who was a night-shift worker at the time, had to change his hours in order to be around for the kids in the evenings, while I tramped the streets losing a big wedge of his salary. Our bills were no cheaper, our mortgage rate was not reduced. Had I not won, I would have plunged my family into a huge amount of debt all for nothing.

On one occasion my opponent accused me of encouraging people to move to Birmingham to get more benefits. It seems to me that the connotation of this, although unsaid, was that I was getting migrants to move here to take benefits away from local people. This was dog-whistle politics designed to send out a message to constituents that I was more interested in outsiders than I was in them. Nasty stuff. His justification for this claim, should he need one, came from a speech I had made about how it was important that council tax benefit schemes should cater for women fleeing domestic violence who had to move across local authority boundaries.

The austerity policies of the then government meant that local councils were having to put in place habitual residency tests to ration whom they would offer benefits and services to. So basically put, if you wanted a council house in Birmingham, or council tax benefit, you had to prove you had lived in the city for a certain period. This policy is incredibly dangerous for victims of domestic violence, who often have to move far away from their homes in order to be safe. To refuse benefits to women fleeing violence puts them at huge risk and would deter many from trying to escape. In my speech I gave examples of families I had worked with who had had to be moved to Birmingham, and suggested that any civilised society would exempt these families from this rule. My opponent, however, decided to present what I was saying as if I was welcoming hordes of people into Birmingham at the cost of the local population. In his frankly unreadable blog, he said I was wrong to encourage benefits tourism. He used words like 'they' to talk about people moving to the city, and banged on about France and how the French should look after their own problems. Which is weird, because I was talking about people from the next Midlands town along, not France!

This is politics right out of the Nigel Farage and Donald Trump playbook. Facts matter not a jot; it is feelings (usually hatred) that count. Describing efforts to protect victims of violence and their children as benefits tourism is despicable and illiberal. Incidentally, Mr Hemming, if you are reading this – which no doubt you are, in order to find salacious things to put on future leaflets – you were on the wrong side of this argument. The Child Poverty Action Group, working with a victim of domestic violence who had to move across local borders, won their case in the High Court in Birmingham, where Justice Hickinbottom (what a name) ruled that the two-year residency rule was unlawful on six separate grounds. The judge stated that the council (Sandwell) acted outside its statutory powers and that the two-year rule was irrational and discriminated on grounds of race and gender.

It doesn't matter if the law – and, frankly, common decency and humanity – is on your side; your political opponents can dress up what you say to get out a message that the *Daily Mail* would be proud of. Never more than in an election campaign are politics and truth such unhappy bedfellows.

So yes, there were times when campaigning was horrific. There were times when I thought that who I was and what I stood for would cost me victory, and with it, thousands of pounds in lost income and years of effort.

All over the world every day there are women who feel guilty for something that someone has done to them. We're trained as women to regret our decisions. The pregnant woman whose boss is discriminating against her will withdraw from making a claim because it might cause the company to lose money and she couldn't live with others losing their jobs. The young girl who thinks she led a boy on because she fancied him and said she would go for a walk with him blames herself when he gropes her and then calls her frigid. For many women the moment our wombs are inhabited we will find any excuse to feel guilty. Did I feed them too much salt? Should I have breastfed for longer? Should I have worked less? The idea that I was, and am, putting my family at risk by doing my job is an ever-present fear I have to fight. Not just the risk of violence from those who oppose me, but the risk of my marriage breaking up, the risk of us losing our livelihood at the whim of a political tide, the risk that my sons will be teased for my profession, or will stumble across pages and pages on YouTube of people who literally hate me. For women, striving often comes with the downside of feeling as if you are letting people down. Your family, your friends, the people who believed in you, they all have a stake in your brand, and it feels heavy on your shoulders.

So here is my handy guide to stop you feeling these things.

Do you think your dad ever punished himself like this?

Close your eyes, imagine you are a kid again and think about your dad sat eating his cheese sandwiches at lunchtime at work. Do you think he was thinking about how awful he was for not being on the school run; do you think he was obsessing over the fact that he might have missed your school nativity play, which was exactly the same as the nativity play you'd performed for the past three years on the trot? Do you think your dad, in his moments of downtime at work, was self-flagellating about how doing his job was a massive risk to your family life? Or instead was he idly wondering how England were doing in the cricket, or whether he had remembered to leave a quid out for the pools man? Now that you have ascertained that your dad was not sat self-loathing while he ate his lunch, ask yourself this question: do you hate your dad? Of course you don't hate him; you remember him largely fondly and thought he was doing a good job for your family. Just like you are.

Ask the people you feel so guilty about what they think

I used to feel such a terrible burden on all the hopeful Labour Party volunteers who turned up in the lashing rain to do menial tasks at the weekend. I used to think, Oh my God, what if all their effort is for nothing? Their disappointment will be all my fault and they will hate me and call me a terrible, time-wasting witch. When I used to occasionally share this with any of them, they'd always find a positive spin on it, saying things like 'We'll know we did the best we could and we will still feel pride.' No one ever called me a waste of space, or was in anyway begrudging.

Word of caution on this one: be wary of asking your kids for their views. My kids are not at all bothered that I work so hard; that is, until they want a new bike or to stay up late, or if I am telling them off about their behaviour. As soon as that happens, they get all 'I just miss you so much, Mom.' Beware of naked self-interest from your younglings, and remind yourself that when you call them from a late-night session at work, they can't even be arsed to turn Minecraft off for one minute to engage in anything other than a monosyllabic conversation with you.

Me: How was school, darling?
Son: Good
Me: What was good?
Son: Dunno
Me: What are you up to?
Son: Yeah, bye, Mom, love you.

Sounds like they're really cut up that I am away at work. Oh yeah, and remember it was your money that bought that sodding computer, so in actual fact you *do* only have yourself to blame.

It's really, really boring for your loved ones if you are racked with self-doubt all the time. People always look better when they smile. No one in the world wants to go for a pint with the person who scrutinises themselves to within an inch of their life. The reason you are reading this book is because you think I've got a bit of get up and go and I present myself as confident and self-assured. Being confident and self-assured, even if it is a veneer, makes the people around you happier and therefore assuages your guilt.

When I have my moments of deep, dark anxiety – and believe you me I have them – I ask my husband a million questions about how awful I am. I seem to want to push him to hate me. I ask him things like 'Do you hate that I'm always out campaigning, that I'm never here? Do you hate it? Do you? DO YOU? Do you hate it?' His response is always 'The only thing I hate is this conversation. Frankly, I'd rather you were out campaigning than here moaning at me about how you're out campaigning all the time.'

Give yourself a break from all the guilt

The truth of course is that you are your own greatest critic, and most of the people you put at risk go there with you of their own volition. If they heard the voice in your head, they would say, 'Don't be such a self-centred loser, it's not all about you. Stop moaning and get on with it.'

There are lots of reasons why I won that election in 2015. Firstly, I was up against a Liberal Democrat. If anyone wants a lesson in how not to seem sincere and genuine, my advice would be to make a really big fuss about an issue – say, the cost of university tuition fees. Make up a load of signs saying how much you hate it and go round the country with those signs like a tourist on a coach trip, having your picture taken. Convince people to believe in your honesty and integrity and your heartfelt views. Then, the second you have the chance to do something about it, do the exact opposite and make tuition fees more expensive. It is tantamount to me suddenly saying, sod this women's rights lark. I've got a shot at a big job; I'll forget that I cared about that. So yeah, the Liberal Democrats can take a bow for helping me win my seat.

The Labour Party gave me love and support and

helped me run the best campaign I could, so I can thank them too. And finally – and I'll take a big deep breath before I say this, because even a publicity-hungry, loud-mouthed, cocky upstart like me finds it tough – I won because I was a really good candidate. I won because I convinced hundreds of hard-working activists to give thousands of hours to help the people in Birmingham Yardley see that I was just like them and that I believed in what was best for them. I won because I was able to communicate with the people I met and allow them to see *me*, not just a shirt in a suit. Most of the votes I won were because of national swing, but there were definitely thousands who thought they wanted to give me a go. I won because I worked really hard to achieve my dream. I won because I believed that I deserved to win and I was able to get other people to believe it too.

THE TRUTH ABOUT
MOTHERHOOD

Since I have been a Member of Parliament, I have attended debates, meetings, scrutiny sessions and rallies about the stubborn little issue of the gender pay gap. The gap between what men and women aged under forty earn is narrowing, due in no small part to the overall reduction of men's wages after the recession of 2008. I've listened to government MPs herald the reduction in the gender pay gap as a real success of theirs, but let's be honest, the fact that it is getting better because men are earning less rather than women earning more isn't really the point. For women over forty the gap widens again, leaving these women still earning as little as 75p for every pound a man earns. The single biggest reason for the gender pay gap is because we women do the lion's share of the work in populating the world. A womb tax, if you will.

In one particular debate in the Commons on this subject, MPs from all parties stood up and talked about their daughters, stating their commitment to ending the gender pay gap because the fruits of their loins were of the female variety: 'I should perhaps follow my honourable friend's declaration of interests by declaring that I have three daughters.' It became girl-child one-upmanship; we could market a DVD of the debate as a drinking game, a Jägerbomb to match the number of daughters mentioned. I can assure you you will be drunk by the end.

I rose to my feet to speak on the subject. It's amazing that I found a way to care, seeing as I have no daughters at all. I am an outlier in my family – there hasn't been a girl baby born since me in 1981. My family and that of my husband are boy producers. So I found myself in a debate with no daughter to lean on for rhetoric's sake. As is my way, I started my speech with a slightly clumsy statement to show how my own household's gender pay gap had been affected by the birth of my children: 'After leaving university, I had the misfortune of having two children.' Context is king. Of course what I meant by 'misfortune' was that the birth of my children had immediately cut my wages and affected my earnings. This is a fact. My children literally made me have less fortune.

The facts aside, what some people heard when I said this was that I hated my children, and wished to sell them to the highest bidder so that I could resume my avaricious life. This is not a fact. Some people heard that I hated my children because they are boys, because I am a feminazi who only likes girls and who wept at their births because of their extended genitals. Again, not a fact. I did cry at their births, but mainly because one of them weighed 10 lb 10 oz. You too would cry if you gave birth to a baby the size of an average two-month-old.

I received letters, emails and hundreds of below-the-line comments on online newspaper articles about how I was a bad mom. My poor dear children were sympathised with for having been born to such a cruel specimen as me who cared more about my wages than their miraculous existence. Forget the gas bill, ladies! Don't worry about paying the mortgage. No, once you have emptied your womb of new life you should walk this earth in the ethereal light of motherhood and survive only on the warm glow that it provides. I've tried to pay my phone bill with warm glow. Alas, it is not a currency currently recognised by Virgin Media.

Before I was elected to Parliament, when I was just a candidate, people would ask me on a daily basis, 'But what about your kids?' or 'What does your husband think about this?' The latter was often said in a slightly accusatory manner, as if I hadn't told him and the questioner was going to ring him and grass on me immediately – 'Your fine fellow of a husband will hear of this, you vixen.' In truth, my husband thought very little about it at all. You might have got a shrug and an eye roll out of him at a push.

After I was elected, in the very first interview I did on my local radio station, I was asked, 'How are you going to cope with your kids?' It was almost as if I hadn't thought about the fact that becoming an MP would mean that I had to live away from my children for three days a week and only now, with the help of very wise news broadcasters, had I realised the enormity of becoming an elected representative. My answer was simple and curt: 'Would you ask me that if I were a male MP with children?' Since then I have been asked this question hundreds of times. Just for sport and in order to point out to whoever is asking that it is a bit sexist, I like to mix up my answers: 'Oh, those aren't my children, I just hired them from an agency to make me look human on the leaflets.' The most honest answer I give on the subject is: 'I'll cope with my children exactly as I did before I was an MP, very badly.'

The truth about motherhood for me is completely different from the truth about motherhood for the next person. It has sometimes been painful and hard, but also matched with euphoria and pride. Most of the time – if I am completely honest – it is unremarkable, tedious and frankly a bit meh. My husband and I had our children when we were relatively young, so we are often called on for wise counsel by our friends who find themselves about to become parents. My husband, in his cynical drawl, usually answers that having children is brilliant and heartbreaking in equal measure; for every happy moment there is one of equal pain, so, and I quote, 'you might as well have not bothered'.

My first son, Harry, was born when I was twenty-three. I'd only been with my boyfriend Tom (now my husband) for a month when he was conceived. Cue the hundreds of jokes I have heard over the past eleven years that I trapped Tom, or the nudge, nudge, wink, wink 'Are you sure he's yours?' comments, made worse by the fact that Tom is dark-skinned and black-haired while Harry looks like the result of an Aryan eugenics programme. The first time I ever met my mother- and father-in-law, I was ten weeks pregnant with their grandchild. Awkward! To those who have a ten-point life plan (if in fact these people actually exist), my decision to have Harry may seem like a rash one. For me it was one of the simplest choices I ever made. I knew the second that test revealed two blue lines that I wanted to have this baby. I pretended, like any self-respecting woman with a new boyfriend would, that I was weighing up the options. I spoke to my own mom, who came from an era when having your first baby at twenty-three meant you were a geriatric mother. When I told her that I was worried I wasn't ready, she replied with a certain degree of flippancy, 'Don't be ridiculous, bab, you will never be ready; now's as good a time as any.'

In my late teens I had suffered from pelvic inflammatory disease and the doctors suspected I had endometriosis. At nineteen they told me I would probably struggle to have children. I wish I could say that at the time I brushed this off as no biggie. I didn't. I was devastated and shocked. When you come from a big boisterous family like I do, having kids seemed an inevitability. I was heartbroken. I know now that having children is absolutely not the be-all and end-all of a woman's life. I have friends who have actively chosen never to have children, and they are happy and fulfilled and seem to get far more holidays in the Caribbean than I'm getting.

But when I was nineteen, I thought I was a failure. I thought the only reason I was put on this earth was to spawn new me's. My body had let me down and I felt completely and utterly useless. Bear in mind that these problems were partly self-inflicted. On one occasion at the Birmingham Women's Hospital, trying to break the ice while chatting to the elderly male gynaecologist in a double-breasted pin-striped suit while he inserted various tools in me, I asked, 'Why did this happen to me?' It feels as if I am making this up now, but I swear the answer I received was 'All I can say, my dear, is that I have never met a nun with these problems.'

Between this moment and the moment I found out I was pregnant with Harry, I felt worthless. I set about abusing my body in any way I could. I felt as if all the people trying to tell me that drinking, smoking, partying and not eating would mess me up in the future didn't realise that as far as I was concerned I had little future to face. My body didn't need to be looked after for a tomorrow that would never come. It had had one purpose and it had failed, so it could take all the abuse I could throw at it. Obviously I was not conscious of this at the time; it is only on reflection that I can see how self-destructive I was. Back then, I just thought I was having a good time.

When I found out I was pregnant with Harry, I was

euphoric, not because I was excited about being a mom, but because I felt for the first time in years that I was worth something. I was terrified about motherhood in practical terms – I am from that generation that the Labour government spent millions of pounds scaring out of throwing their lives away having babies as teenagers. I'd played with enough crying doll aids in school health classes to make me realise babies were a bit of a nuisance. The being-a-mom bit was completely alien to me; I was just happy that I would matter in the world again.

I'm certain that the connection between adoptive parents and their children is exactly the same as for those who have them the traditional way. However, before I actually had a baby, I really believed that there was some cosmic bond between a birth mom and her baby that could never be replicated. There are children in my life now to whom I am no blood relation, but I would walk across knives for them. It takes a village to raise a child; everybody has that favourite auntie or uncle who is no relation whatsoever to them. My Auntie Pat, who was my dad's mate from school, still rings me when exciting things happen in my life, and I become immediately childlike. My husband has Auntie Liz, who describes him as her surrogate son. My children have a whole cast of oddly shaped guardians. Matt and Adam, a couple who used to lodge in our house, are the people they regard as their replacement parents; when they were little, they charmingly referred to this gay couple, without realising the gag, as 'Madam'.

Because I had not fallen pregnant with Harry on purpose, I was hell-bent on planning my second baby. I wanted to know what it felt like to decide to have a baby and then get pregnant. I wanted to have the grown-up rather than the gymslip-mom experience. Turns out it felt exactly the same. I love my children so much it actually hurts, but the idea of a cosmic connection between me and them is bogus. Their dad loves them just as much, and I suspect their nan loves them even more.

What I know now – what I was too young and self-indulgent to realise when I was nineteen – is that women and men who don't have children matter just as much as those that do. Every week when I am out knocking doors like a dutiful constituency MP, I meet single people or couples without kids who feel that they are ignored by Westminster. The constant rhetoric about hard-working families makes them feel like they don't exist. I can totally understand why. Our policy-making and much of our government spending is earmarked for 1950s family ideals. If you are a single-income household without kids, aside from the NHS, which you probably use less, and the basic council services like bins and street lights, there always seems to be less given to you. I try to console these people with the fact that they didn't have to watch *Finding Nemo* eight times in one day with a three-year-old with whooping cough; people like me who receive (or received before the Tories took it away) universal child benefit have to take the rough with the smooth. It is little comfort. We have got to find a way to create policy with matching rhetoric that doesn't keep dragging us backwards to the ideal of family values. The last decade has seen some shifts in the realisation that a family is not just made up of a man and a woman, but still so many are left feeling that society is not built for them.

This is one of the reasons why I am an advocate of the idea of a universal basic income for everyone, regardless of whether you have 2.4 children or you live on your own with seventeen cats. As someone who lived on welfare benefits when my children were little, I am constantly riled by the distinction made in Parliament between taxpayers and benefit claimants. They are the same thing; they are not two distinct groups who can be pitted against each other. I always worked and paid tax even when my children were tiny, but I needed child benefit and child tax credits to help to pay for childcare and to make it worth my while to keep working. If everyone received some universal benefit from the government, we could stop the 'othering' of people on benefits; we could stop people who don't have children feeling like they get nothing; we could all be in the same boat. At the moment, it feels like we are not just not in the same boat, we are in fact the cad from *Titanic* who takes a seat in the lifeboat from women and children because he thinks he matters more.

My experience of barren hopelessness as a teenager is the reason I hate listening to the lazy rhetoric about women having babies just to get benefits. The Conservative government is rolling out a two-child policy – only paying child tax credits to the first two children born in a household. This stems from and feeds the myth that girls have babies for council flats. I know that the reason poor, vulnerable or mixed-up young women have babies is not for an extra £69 a week; they have them because being a mom makes you feel like you matter; it gives you worth. For thousands and thousands of women every year, the birth of a child makes them count in a world that calls them scroungers, thick, slags, sluts, useless, doll or 'I'll have my tea with two sugars, darling.' Being called Mom, Mum, Mam, Ma makes you feel like you belong.

I'm not proud of this. I'm not happy that women today still feel that the only thing about them that matters is their fertility. Arguably the only thing harder than being a mother working in politics is to be a childless woman in Parliament. I was dismayed by comments made by smug-mum MP Andrea Leadsom about the now prime minister Theresa May not having a stake in the future because she is childless. What an absolute load of old rubbish. I was delighted that we have come far enough that this nineteenth-century throwback rhetoric was one of the final nails in the coffin of Leadsom's leadership bid. Are we supposed to imagine for a second that in a moment of national crisis, when Theresa May has to make a life-and-death judgement call, she is going to think, 'Ah, who cares, blow up the country. After all, it's not like I've got any kids to worry about'? I may not agree with Mrs May on most things, but I feel fairly certain that she is not on a trajectory to damn the future because she happens not to have biological offspring.

Mind you, it is not the worst thing Supermum Leadsom said when discussing her oh-so-wise outlook on child-rearing. When asked about men being child carers she said, 'Your odds are stacked against you if you employ a man. We know paedophiles are attracted to working with children. I'm sorry, but they're the facts.' And people call *me* a man hater. My husband has pretty much been the primary child carer for our family since our kids were born. Both of my children went to nurseries where men were employed, and today they continue to have male teachers. Andrea Leadsom should jolly well know better – she is a government minister! The sad truth is that in the UK and around the world the crazy idea that women are somehow some sort of saintly child lovers, while men shouldn't be caring for children – for many reasons, weirdly amongst them because statistically speaking they are probably perverts – is surprisingly still the norm.

I'm just not sure why our gendered views on parenting persist. When I was pregnant, I was told that I would find a new Jerusalem upon giving birth. I used to put my hands on my belly and desperately try to feel something other than fat and tired. I'd been led to believe that when I actually gave birth I'd have a rush of love so overwhelming I would weep tears of joy. What I actually felt was fear. Real fear for the first time in my life. For weeks, I was just relieved that I'd got through the day without anyone dying. Also, no one tells you when you have your first baby that in the days afterwards you will bleed huge clots. I wish someone *had* told me, because the terror that comes over you when you go to the toilet and think your kidneys have fallen out is not the best way to start the supposed most magical time in your life.

I love my kids. I love being a mom – I love being *their* mom – but I also recognise that the way we put motherhood on a pedestal is holding both women and men back. I don't think women are better parents than men. Aside from the issue of women taking some time off to recover from labour and to breastfeed the baby, there is absolutely no reason why fathers shouldn't be entitled to exactly the same parental leave. Public policy still dictates that parenting is mothers' work. In the UK, mothers are entitled to one year off work; the state or your employer will provide you with nine months' maternity pay. Dad gets the same for only two weeks. In recent times, the government legislated that men and women could share the nine months' pay a woman was entitled to. Only 2 per cent of UK fathers have taken this up. In Sweden, fathers can choose to share their parental leave equally with their partner and receive an 'equality bonus' for doing so. The more days that are divided equally between the parents, the higher the bonus. Men are incentivised to share the care and families are not left poorer if dads (sadly still usually the higher earners) take the time off. Guess what? More dads in Sweden do this. When you study gender equality as much as I do, you become accustomed to feeling shamed by Scandinavian countries. I want to live in a world where both parents are offered nine months off and they can take it either consecutively or concurrently (if they have any sense).

For some reason, we all sign up to the idea that women are doing something sacred in a baby's first year that no one else could manage. I was mainly crying and eating six Bakewell tarts in one sitting, which to be fair is a habit my son has picked up. It came too late for me, but women are starting to admit how hard, mind-numbing and demoralising parenting an infant can be. Mothers do that terrible thing of constantly comparing themselves to other moms or some non-existent gold standard. We diminish how difficult things are by scolding ourselves that others have it worse; at least our babies are happy and healthy. I wish that we could all feel what we feel and know that that is OK, even when we are sometimes so tired, so undervalued and so bored that the thought crosses our minds that having children at all might have been a mistake.

With my second son, Danny, I went back to work when he was six weeks old and he is one of the happiest, most robust and self-assured kids I have ever met. Between me, his dad, his grandparents and the nursery, we raised him just fine. Their upbringing – whilst not perfect – has meant that my kids have a realistic view of the kind of family life they should expect. I remember watching *The Great British Bake Off* with my elder son. Some high-flying businesswoman who was taking part was talking about her kids and how she likes to bake with them. Her video introduction ended with the statement 'I just don't know how I do it all.' My son looked at me, rolled his eyes and said, 'Duh ... childcare.' This moment of sarcastic inflection made me incredibly proud to be his mom.

We all still have so far to come in how we view the gender roles of parenting. Those of us who read the *Guardian* and are married to modern metrosexual men pat ourselves on the back as if old-fashioned traditional outlooks are something that other people suffer from. Whenever I talk about the gender pay gap, men tell me how their liberated wives earn much more than them, or women tell me that their husbands are the carers and have 'let' them be the breadwinners. The middle classes think of the working class as a place where women are baby machines and men are out bending metal or driving something to bring in the crust. It seems to me that the middle classes are kidding themselves if they think they are any better. Educated middle-class women are often the ones writing articles or presenting TV shows about how they love to bake and craft and still fit in being a mummy. They are still shackled to motherhood as their role.

My family is as guilty as any. Not long ago, sat in a café with my son, we picked up a newspaper and started to flick through it. There was a news story about the son of a Member of Parliament being attacked in a takeaway, and Harry turned to me and asked, 'Do you know this man, Mommy, the MP whose son was attacked?' I quickly scanned the story and realised that the MP in question was not a man, as my son had assumed, but was in fact Lady Victoria Borwick, the member for Kensington and Chelsea. This is a common mistake that people make: they hear a job title and they automatically see either a man or a woman in that role. Doctor = man, nurse = woman. When my son saw the title MP, he imagined a man, even though the only MP he knows is a woman. This a kid raised by feminist parents. You might imagine this makes me want to slam my head against a brick wall. What hope do all the people not raised by feminist MPs have if my own son got this wrong?

The idea that motherhood is sacred and that women's bodies are some kind of virtuous temple of creation has left many women in heartbreaking despair. Every day mothers painfully compare their bodies, their birth experiences, their parenting to that of their peers. Even the cynical, 'I'm so laid-back', cocksure mothers like me feverishly benchmark our parenting against other people. I am not sure my husband and I would have had anything to talk about when our kids were toddlers if we hadn't constantly – critically – pored over the decisions our friends had made about their children. It happens before they are even born, in middle-class circles at least. Women moon over the idea of having the most natural birth, casting shade on others who don't manage it. I know all the statistics about how natural birth is safer and better and how breast is best, but up and down the country new moms are weeping over the heads of their newborns because they can't get the hang of breastfeeding and have for some reason been led to believe by some crappy meme on Facebook that if they give them baby formula they will basically be feeding them crack.

My own mother was a proper baby warrior – a 1970s National Childbirth Trust champion and a women's liberation member of La Leche League (which I think is a bit like Team America for breastfeeders, or at least that's what it sounds like). I tried to have my first baby at home because of my liberated heritage. I thought that because my mom could pop out babies without breaking a sweat I would be able to as well. Turns out my son had the cord around his neck and frankly was as awkward in birth as he is in life. I was rushed to hospital in an ambulance after eighteen hours of having contractions every minute, but it was not the pain that made me weep; it was the disappointment that I had failed to have a natural birth without drugs. I cried into my mother's chest and told her I had let her down. Women's liberation fanatic aside, my mother was a plain-speaking working-class woman and her response was simply 'Don't be so bleedin' daft.'

I was definitely guilty at the age of twenty-three of playing mommy superiority, as if the decisions I was making had any bearing on the way other people produced, raised, fed, weaned, schooled and ultimately ignored their children. The moment I realised it was all for naught was in May 2008, when I was five months pregnant with my enormous second baby. This baby was planned, not by me and Tom, you understand, but by me and my girlfriends. After your first baby is born, if you are lucky you find some like-minded women to hang out with who are off work at the same time as you. My gaggle of mom friends became so close that four out of five of us got pregnant within six months of each other so that we could sneakily drink wine (post-birth) together in the park while on maternity leave.

Fertility was on our side, and we were all fat with baby. We often shared our fears about the births and we all had varying ideas about how clinical the process was going to be. Jess, who lives in the house opposite me, was due first. On 15 May 2008, she gave birth to baby Iris, perfect in every way except one. When Jess's labour had started, her baby's placenta had got something wrong, and Iris had taken her first breath while she was still all warm inside her mom, which meant that she drowned. In all those conversations we had had, silently judging each other's childbirth choices, none of us had even contemplated that one of our babies would not be coming home from the hospital.

We remember Iris every year; the children we were incubating to be her friends dance around the tree we dedicated to her in the park. Jess and Iris taught me that we should never be snobby, self-righteous and pious about birth and motherhood, because so what if I had an epidural, my baby came home. That is all that matters.

So many of our views on parenthood come from old-fashioned ideas about marriage. Women are fed a fantasy about romance rather than partnership. I don't want the Milk Tray Man to scale a building and leave chocolates for me while I'm sleeping; I want him to remember to take the bins out. My marriage is a partnership with a bolt-on of romance. Every woman I know has sat by while one of her colleagues received a bouquet of flowers at the office from their beloved. We have all felt jealous of these moments, even though the cynic in me would make some comment about how funny it is that people can only feel really loved if green-eyed onlookers are there to validate it.

My husband has sent me a bunch of flowers at work on only one occasion. I was away at a conference in Manchester just weeks after finding out I was pregnant. We were in the first flush of our relationship. It was clear that Tom had never bought flowers from an Interflora company before and so had no idea how much they cost. He had clearly been upsold by the florist on the phone, and when asked how much he wanted to spend, he must have said, 'I dunno, fifty quid?' What arrived for me was the biggest bouquet of white flowers I have ever seen in my life. They looked more suited to the arrangement that goes on top of a coffin than a romantic bunch of flowers for your newly pregnant girlfriend. They had been left with a security guard at the conference centre, who then brought them up to me. As he handed them over, he said, 'A bunch this size, that's guilt about more than just kissing, love.' That was the beginning and end of our public displays of affection.

Tom is my family, and so our romance is different; for us it is about our partnership. He remembers the things I like when he pops to the corner shop, always coming back with a small treat. He waits until I am back in Birmingham to watch *Game of Thrones*. When I feel guilty about being a crap wife and a crap mom, which is a near-daily occurrence, he reminds me that this is just our life and he is not doing anything particularly special. To this day, I still think that the most romantic thing he has ever done is buy me Tampax when he does the weekly shop. That is real life; that is partnership. This is the stuff wives and mothers do all the time.

My marriage is in no way patriarchal, yet people still treat us as if it is. I remember a senior member of the Labour Party staff congratulating my husband for all that I had achieved – 'We know she couldn't be doing any of this without you.' To this, one of the many comments my husband gets for simply being a dad, he responded, 'My wife's achievements have got absolutely naff all to do with me.' Of course this is not how I feel; I feel like I could do nothing without his support. I feel like my husband is the best goddam husband anyone could have. He supports me without it being a thing; he expects and wants no praise for just being. I don't think he realises quite how rare that is. I do know for a fact, though, that wives of politicians or men who have achieved greatness would never get the same acknowledgement he does.

Few things annoy me more than when people see me out in the evening and ask me, 'Oh, is Tom babysitting?'

No, Tom is not sodding babysitting; he is the father of our children, not a fourteen-year-old trying to earn money to go out and buy a packet of fags and some cider, or whatever it is teenagers do these days. Less so now, but in years gone by, relatives would offer to help him out with the kids if I was away with work, as if he needed a break from being their dad on his own for three days straight. We treat men as if they are completely incapable and mollify them like they are children themselves. My husband is a great dad, but not because he does the school run and cooks the dinner every day; more because he actually likes talking about *Marvel* superheroes and building go-karts. To be fair, he would be doing both of these things had he never had children.

I recognise that I have a good husband. I have an incredibly good father too; in my childhood he was the person who was there when I got home from school and he made my dinner every day except Sunday. My father-in-law takes an equal share with my mother-in-law in providing childcare to help me now I have a crazy London/Birmingham life. To me the examples of good men are everywhere to see. They are not exceptional; they are normal. Good, yes. Extraordinary? No. When I worked at Women's Aid, I was trained to look for signs of physical and psychological abuse. I worried that this would cause me to start hating my husband and other men. In fact, it made me realise that most men are not arseholes.

I am not so puritanical that I can't take the odd sexist

comment from a man without realising that it is the way he lives his life that counts, not the way he might chat with his mates. I am frequently called a man hater by my detractors. I don't hate men at all. I just hate men who beat and rape their wives and girlfriends. Call me fussy, if you will. I don't like men who treat their families as a hobby; I don't like women who do this either, but if I'm being honest, I have only met a few of these, and they were usually deeply vulnerable in one way or another.

I know that men have a really important role to play in women achieving equality, and the very best way to start is by offering them a chance to do that in their families. I won't say be an amazing dad, because that demands praise that women rarely get. All I ask is that you try and be as good a dad as your partner is a mom. Same goes for same-sex or non-binary couples. If one of you is doing more work than the other, stop being such a douche. If men had equal paternity rights and took them, eventually we would stop seeing all mothers as Virgin Marys sent only to spawn other great men. If we were a society truly committed to equal parenting rights and roles, a man in his thirties sat in front of an interview panel would be as much at risk of taking parental leave as his female counterpart. In fact, since men can have babies until they die, if we had completely equal parenting roles and benefits, the only people who wouldn't be a baby risk to an employer would be post-menopausal women, and frankly I'm OK with that because older women are doubly discriminated against. They deserve a break.

Apparently I am a parliamentary poster girl for 'having it all'. I'm a relatively young MP who has a young family and a happy marriage. Neil Coyle, Matthew Pennycook and Conor McGinn were all elected on the same day as me. All are of a similar age to me and all have children, younger and more demanding than mine in fact. I will bet a whole year's salary on the fact that no one has ever asked them how they have it all. I loathe and detest the constant question, 'Can women have it all?' It is probably the most frequently written sentence in the whole history of the printed press, only narrowly beating 'Migrant family lives on £1 million of benefits per week' and 'Can a glass of red wine a day extend your life by five years?' 'Can women have it all?' is as ridiculous a statement as both of these headline winners, but is rarely judged in the same cynical light.

What does having it all actually mean? It is true that over the years, as women have gone back to work, we have failed to give up the other stuff we do. We don't stop doing the washing-up because we have jobs. We don't think, screw taking Gran to the hospital, I have a job, you know. So our having it all often actually means working like slaves day and night and at the weekends to boot. The Office for National Statistics estimated the value of unpaid work in UK homes in 2014 to be £1.019 trillion. That is the equivalent of 56.1 per cent of the UK's national output. So all the childcare, elderly care, cleaning and cooking that women are doing is equivalent to over half of our country's gross domestic product. We women are going to work and then doing a shedload of other stuff that apparently we could have been earning trillions for. This seems like a bad deal, or, if you look at it another way, a business plan for a nice little earner.

The very idea of having it all applies only to women. When men don't have it all, no one comments on it. The brilliant and satirical Twitter account The Man Who Has It All does a fine job poking fun at this idea. Loads of my male friends don't have children, yet no one does the sad-face head tilt at them at weddings and family parties. The famous comparison being between Jennifer Aniston and George Clooney. Both are childless, but while I've read plenty of column inches about the inside of Ms Aniston's uterus, I've never so much as seen a sentence dedicated to investigating Mr Clooney's scrotum. Who decided that having it all was to have children and a job? These are pretty low ambitions we women set for ourselves. I want to be a polymath, a broad, an adventurer, a change-maker. These are ambitions. Being pregnant and employed is not the stuff dreams are made of. I bet if you ask a group of six-year-old girls what they want to be when they grow up, they will not say, 'I'd like to be a moderate wage earner while still having time to care for a family.'

'I've decided not to have children and to focus on my career; I think these days you cannot have both.' These were the words of a twenty-one-year-old woman who came to give evidence to the All-Party Parliamentary Group on Sex Inequality. Immediately my guard was up, as if her statement was somehow an insult to me. I snapped, 'When I was your age, I was one year off falling pregnant with my first baby. Now I am an MP, and I had a pretty good job before that. I'm only thirty-four.' I was affronted by this young woman's seeming lack of ambition to have everything any similarly aged young man could want. Applying the usual test of 'Would a man say this?' the answer is of course no. But I was still wrong to project my experiences onto her. In fact, she was completely right. While sitting on the Women and Equalities Select Committee Enquiry into the gender pay gap, I was depressed in every session by the evidence from big companies and employment institutions that if you take more than six months off, your career is toast. The report of that enquiry clearly states:

> The Institute of Directors and the Family and Childcare Trust were just two of the many organisations which raised the issue of the 'maternity penalty' as a component of the gender pay gap. As the Family and Childcare Trust explain: 'This wage disadvantage is proportionally higher for better qualified women but research suggests that even for women who had GCSE level qualifications or below (Level Two or below) and controlling for other factors, these women's average hourly wages were 14 per cent lower if they had moved in and out of work after having children than if they had a stable career trajectory.'

Turns out I am the exception, not the rule. I shouldn't have told her she was wrong as if we were the same and our experiences would be the same, but I cannot bear the thought of women, especially brilliant, bright young women who have the gumption to give evidence in Parliament, feeling that they have to choose.

The first question any activist who is a mother asks me about being in Parliament is 'Do you think I could do it?' I think I might make a banner to hang in Parliament Square that reads, 'If you think you couldn't do what we are doing in here, you clearly haven't seen some of the people who are managing it.' Male MPs with young children suffer the exact burdens the women do. The only difference is that they don't beat themselves up about it. They are not weighed down by all the questions about how they are coping, or the thousands of magazine articles questioning whether they can have it all.

The fact that I am a mother has both helped and hindered my career. In practical terms, it has meant what it means for most parents: juggling my working hours to make sure that I get to see my children. On the plus side, I have benefited from the fact that people think that because I am a mom I'm more like them, and I have definitely played up to this. For a gentle reminder of how silly this is, we need look no further than the example of Margaret Thatcher. The Iron Lady had two children just as I do, and that is where our similarities end; at least I hope so, otherwise one of my children is going to end up taking part in a failed coup attempt.

Our wombs should neither beatify us nor vilify us; let's face it, the uterus is just an organ that spends 90 per cent of its time being a total pain in the arse. If it wasn't for the fact that I might get osteoporosis, I'd have mine whipped out today. As someone who decided at the tender age of twenty-seven that her baby-making days were over, I'm staring down the barrel of thirty years of pointless periods.

I know the evidence is totally stacked against me when I say this, but I genuinely believe that you can be a good parent and be ambitious and successful as well. The reason I know this is that men have been doing it since the beginning of time.

THE TRUTH ABOUT
BEING HUMAN

I'm guilty of indulging in identity politics. Personality politics plays to my strengths, mainly because I have a personality that I am willing to show. I'm a woman with a regional accent, a couple of kids and a husband who drives a van. I've lived on benefits, I wear big hoop earrings that I buy in pound shops, I've had a proper job doing worthy things and I like trashy Saturday-night telly. Don't be fooled, though. I also like holidays in the south of France, I eat fancy food whenever the opportunity comes up, I sometimes do my shopping in Waitrose and I enjoy going to art galleries (though it is mainly for the gift shops).

I am absolutely no better a politician for all of these things than my colleagues who were deeply steeped in student politics at Oxford and went on to work in government. Or those who were man and boy in the trade union movement. Even, dare I say it, than those who worked in business, big or otherwise. We are all different. We all have our skills and specialist subjects.

Since I was elected, I have been genuinely shocked by how surprised people are that I am 'normal'. I had no idea that being myself would be such a revelation. I almost never realise that what I am saying might cause a storm, either positive or negative. It is fine to be cavalier about speaking up. I wear it as a badge of pride that I dare to say the unsayable. Sometimes I make myself wince at how far I am willing to push it. The result of speaking up is rarely worse than a few angry column inches for a day or two. Until recently, that is. In June 2016, speaking up as an honest, passionate, political woman became dangerous. My friend and colleague Jo Cox was shot and stabbed in the street for daring to be honest about her views. The very fact that she spoke from the heart about the unpopular subject of immigration and refugees cost her her life.

The humanity of politicians was laid bare following Jo's murder. In every tribute paid to her we could see that in fact politicians *are* just like us. They have children, husbands, homes, plans. In my own tribute and also in her family's interviews and her husband's eulogy, we tried not to beatify her. She was a young, beautiful woman; many wanted to see her as a perfect angel. She was not perfect; she was human. Don't get me wrong, she was far and away one of the best humans I will ever meet, but it was her humanity, not some special gift, not some magic knowledge, that made her so exquisite. I know and she knew that every single one of us is capable of being as good as she was. People are excellent; we really don't give them anywhere near as much credit as they deserve. I bloody love people.

Jo and I were proud feminists who fought together. It was not her feminism or even that she was a fellow woman and tired mother in Parliament that made me love her; it was her truly tangible and unguarded normality and humanity. People want to remember her as something special, one of a kind, but I think that misses the point of who she was. Jo and I shared the belief that it takes nothing fancy, no highfalutin school, inherent genius or innate kindness, to be a wonderful person; in fact most humans can be brilliant with few resources other than one another.

For forty-eight hours after Jo died, overtures about a change in politics flooded mainstream and social media. People vowed to respect our representatives and all they do. #ThankyourMP trended on Twitter as the world stopped and considered what representatives actually sacrifice. Three days after Jo's memorial debate in Parliament, the country went to the polls in the divisive binary European Union referendum and everything returned to normal. In fact not normal; things got much worse. Politicians squabbled, some of the public screamed and kicked back, and sure as anything, my social media and my inbox once again filled with people calling me a traitor, a scab, an ugly bitch drinking gravy from the train. #ThankyourMP had a legacy of about twenty-five minutes. The vocal minority swept away the idea of our humanity as quickly as they had lapped it up.

'You're all the same' is one of the most common things you hear when you are masochistic enough to spend your spare time knocking on doors to canvass people's views. The idea that MPs, or in fact anyone in public life, are exactly like you has been on a downward spiral for many years. It doesn't matter that I was elected five years after the MPs' expenses scandal; many people still think that we become MPs for selfish reasons. My humanity, my feelings, my life experiences were stripped away the second I was elected. I became 'the Establishment'. I don't feel any different – slightly more stretched, perhaps – yet people who seem desperate for politicians to be more like them are the ones I have largely found treat me differently. My all-time favourite doorstep discourse went like this:

Me: Hello, I'm Jess Phillips. I'm calling from the local Labour Party. We're out in your area today and wondered if you had any local issues you want to share with us?

Constituent: You're all the same, after one thing, you only come around when there's an election.

Me: Well I'm sorry you feel that way, sir, but in fact there isn't an election for another eighteen months, so really I'm just interested in what you think I should be doing locally.

Constituent: We never see anyone round here, no one bothers with us.

Me: But I am here, here I am, on your doorstep, I do care.

Constituent: No one ever asks our opinions; you
   only care when there's an election.
Me: OK, I just did ask your opinion and we've
   established that there isn't an election, so would
   you like to share anything with me now?
Constituent: You only bother when there's an
   election.

I think it is safe to say I did not convince that fella.

It can sometimes seem that no matter what you do, no matter how hard you try to be at one with the voting public, you can never quite get past the idea that you are somehow 'other'. One Tory MP told me that someone actually asked him, without even a whiff of humour, if he eats swan. I mean, I know the Tories use phrases like 'it really is a smashing little day school', which definitely sounds a bit 'other' to oiks like me (aren't all schools open in the day?), but the idea that they are all munching on swan is, I think, a bit far-fetched. I have in fact eaten a packet of sandwiches in a Co-op café with Jacob Rees-Mogg, the most old-fashioned Tory of all, and I can confirm he did not ask for swan on wholemeal. Actually he looked right at home there, although it is true he was the only person in a double-breasted pin-striped suit.

There is no greater compliment my constituents could ever pay me than saying, 'You're one of us, bab.' I live for those moments. I think that people are sick to death of politicians, CEOs and bigwigs answering questions they weren't asked with well-rehearsed lines. Everybody does this at times, even me. The truth I have come to realise in Westminster is that almost all of the people sitting there are very human. Some of them are side-splittingly funny, but I have also watched MPs weep in the corridors because their kids are being bullied at school. I've watched them run out of the chamber shaking with uncontrollable emotion because of the decline or decimation of their constituency's biggest employer. During the steel crisis, when thousands of people's jobs were on the line, I watched their representatives bleed their desperation on the floor of the corridors of power. I've offered a crafty calm-down fag to more than one MP who was about to lose their rag over an issue they felt helpless about.

Meg Hillier, the chair of the Public Accounts Committee, once found me literally weeping in the corridor of the committee floor of the House of Commons, after a now famous moment of frustration at a meeting of the PLP about women's diminishing place in our party. She still grabs me now when she sees I am bubbling up and invites me for a sneaky sit-down in her office, a glass of something and an opportunity to howl at the moon in a private place. We all need someone around to snap us out of a rut or carry us along when we are crowd-surfing through a success. Whatever we do in life, doing it alone is rarely fruitful and it's never fun.

During late-night sessions in the House, when we are there sometimes until dawn, MPs can get fairly introspective. I have shared some deep, dark woes with my friends and colleagues in those small hours. The trouble is, when the world finally gets to see these woes, it is usually at a crisis point, when some massive gaffe has occurred or things in your personal life have got out of hand. We are rarely given the same leniency in these moments as people would give their friends and neighbours. My grandma used to say, 'Over here there is sorrow and shame, over the road they're feeling the same.' If the person over the road holds public office, we give them no such empathy.

If we want people to be more authentic and represent us better, we have got to be more tolerant when they mess up. We have got to give them the benefit of the doubt. Politicians, CEOs and managers all over the country are sat weeping in their offices. When they step in front of a camera, a canteen full of workers, or a staff meeting, they usually deliver the lines. They act their best professional self, because doing anything else would open them up to massive criticism. The House of Commons is absolutely packed full of personalities, humans, comedians and charmers, although from 99 per cent of television appearances you wouldn't know it.

I have never been very good at politician-speak. Every day people tell me how unprofessional I seem on the telly, or if they are at the receiving end of a tongue-lashing on Twitter. Apparently if you are an MP, you are meant to take abuse and ill-informed vitriol lying down. As best I can tell, this is akin to being the slightly plain girl in a Jane Austen novel, expected to sit quietly and demurely while my parents discuss with their betters how unmarriageable I am. Well sod that. If you have a pop at me and you are just being mean, expect a response and don't moan when you get one. If you are a Tory MP and you say something disgusting about the behaviour of 'benefits scroungers', migrants, single parents or whoever we are demonising this week, expect a bollocking. If you are a Labour MP and you say something sexist, don't think my tribal tendencies won't make me roll my eyes and tut before calling you out. Sod being professional in the face of ass-hattery. Don't insult me, my constituents, my family or my friends and then shriek like a baby about how unprofessional I am when I make you look a fool.

On one occasion when I was scrutinising the Conservatives' Welfare and Work Bill in committee, I had to keep reminding the Tory ministers in front of me that they were wrongly making a distinction between tax payers and benefits claimants. Everyone pays some sort of tax, and most people at some point in their lives will also receive benefits. I pointed out that pensioners were benefits claimants and taxpayers; I pointed out that George Osborne, then Chancellor of the Exchequer, had spoken of how his family had received child benefit even after he moved into his grace-and-favour home at 11 Downing Street. I asked them over and over again to stop making this false distinction, a device intended to sow hatred and division, to make everyone think their neighbour is getting more than they are, and ultimately to incite selfishness and breed Tory votes. In a feeble attempt at a come-back, Shailesh Vara, an Under Secretary of State in Her Majesty's Government, told me, 'We need to treat this debate as though it was taking place in Parliament, not in a sixth-form debating society.' He basically called me an unprofessional child for doing my job, which was to scrutinise line by line the government's representation of their Bill.

I tell you what is not professional: on the same Bill committee, every time a vote was called (in Bill committees, votes are called every time the committee finishes debating a clause or an amendment), the Conservative whip had to hold up a piece of paper to show the Conservative members how to vote, in case they got it wrong. Bear in mind there are only three options: aye, no, or no vote. If in my old job my boss had had to hold up a sign to remind me whether to say yes or no, I'm guessing we would have looked less than professional. I think even members of a sixth-form debating society can follow the thread of a debate well enough to know which way to vote without the head boy or girl writing it down on a piece of paper for them. Honestly, Westminster is a baffling place at times.

So because I talk back, because I speak up, because I don't use exclusive language, I am apparently unprofessional. I try my best to speak in the Commons or on telly as I would to my constituents. I try to answer questions and be myself. Within reason, of course. In normal conversations I don't have to thank the Speaker or the chair every fifteen seconds. When serving on a Bill committee, or taking part in a debate in Westminster Hall (the smaller of the Commons chambers), everybody always says before they speak, 'Thank you, Madam/ Mr Chairman, it is a pleasure to serve under your chairmanship.' It is safe to say I don't do that around the kitchen table. I like to mix it up by saying Chair instead of Chairman, Ms Deputy Speaker instead of Madam. Seriously, who says Madam? I'm fairly certain that the Deputy Speakers are not doling out wages in a brothel. Saying Ms instead of Madam is about as subversively feminist as the conventions of the House of Commons allow. Even that raises eyebrows.

I am determined to carry on speaking with my own voice. I don't do it just because it saves me having to learn all the fancy conventions; I also do it because I know that unless we start sounding like the public, ordinary people will disengage from politics and we'll be left with the Establishment holding court, and we can't have that! It is easy for me to act jolly and human. It is OK for members of the party in opposition to give their actual opinions when grilled on *Newsnight*. It is much tougher to deliver the government line, so I will cut government MPs some slack.

People have commented on my accessibility. Julie Burchill said that spending time with me talking politics had 'the tantalising tang of bunking off', while Rachel Cooke wrote in the *Guardian*, 'Perhaps it really is possible for our legislators to look, sound and even act like us, and yet still have our best interests at heart.' Obviously I am touched by all the lovely comments, but for everyone who likes me, there is the chorus of the alternative. 'How

did you ever become an MP, you are so unprofessional.'
'Jess Phillips speaking like a common old fishwife again, I
suppose we get what we deserve from our representatives.'
'People say she is a breath of fresh air, she's nothing more
than Labour's answer to Katie Hopkins.' I'm not sure Ms
Hopkins would appreciate the comparison, and I'm also
not sure she would appreciate being called Ms Hopkins.
Recently I attended a party to celebrate seventy years of
Radio 4 *Women's Hour*. When I arrived, they couldn't find
my badge, so as a gag they gave me the one that was
intended for Katie Hopkins. It is now one of my most
treasured possessions.

The trouble is, speaking with your own voice means
that you can easily get into trouble. Every time I type a
tweet, write a column, rise to my feet in the Chamber, I
am weighed down by the desire to not cause a massive
shit storm. It happens without me ever realising it was
going to, although self-righteous naysayers love to say that
I did it for the publicity. Turns out I am actually a terrible
judge of what will capture the nation's imagination, or at
least the imagination of the nation's pundits. I have
absolutely no outrage radar.

My most exposing experience of this was when I was
asked on *Question Time* about the events of New Year's
Eve 2015 in Cologne, where crowds of women were
assaulted en masse, seemingly by newly settled refugees.
At the time there was a great deal of moral outrage about
this, and rightly so. The trouble was that much of the
debate had been hijacked by people suggesting that

these events were the by-product of the settlement of refugees from Islamic countries. I rather clumsily said that the events were awful and we had to do more to integrate the cultural norms of newly arrived refugees and migrants. The trouble was, I refused to bow down to the idea that violence against women is something that is brought to our shores by migrants. It isn't. There are hundreds of women sexually assaulted every week across the UK, and there always have been. I went on to say that the events in Cologne could be compared to a night out in Birmingham's Broad Street. Perhaps I shouldn't have been so geographically specific. But I'm a Birmingham girl, so I gave a Birmingham example. The same sort of groping, cat-calling and abuse probably happens in every boozy night-time economy in the UK.

The following day was spent watching painfully as newspaper report after newspaper report rehashed the story, with varying degrees of accuracy and sympathy for my point. I was accused of not caring about what had happened in Cologne, which is frankly ridiculous given that I am a well-known feminist anti-violence campaigner. I was painted as a traitor to my city: again totally ridiculous and funnily enough by hardly anyone from Birmingham. My phone rang every five minutes with requests for me to go on this telly programme or that radio show. The horror of watching the national consciousness wake up to me was made all the more difficult by the fact that I hadn't got to bed until 3 a.m., and while my phone was ringing off the hook, I was traipsing through the mud of

Sheldon Country Park with the RSPB looking for a dunnock, a bird that did not seem to want to be found. It seems a ridiculous juxtaposition, but on reflection it was a fair representation of the media frenzy. I think back and laugh at how Alan Partridge it was, not dissimilar to the scene where he is trying to film a promotional video about canals and the farmers appear and drop a cow on him.

I declined all media requests bar my local radio station, who basically doorstepped me while I was in the city centre. I wasn't interested in being on the telly, which I'm sure would shock all those who think I only have opinions to increase my profile.

The Cologne/Broad Street debacle was a moment when a rehearsed line would have got my point across much better. My friend the lovely Polly Billington, who gives great advice on such matters, had warned me about what she calls 'committing news'. There are times when I definitely should just keep my mouth shut; as a friend once said: 'You just missed the perfect opportunity to say nothing.' Sometimes I worry that eventually the fear of inadvertently causing controversy will weigh so heavily on me that I will just stop speaking my mind. Other times, I am sure I will learn a way to be myself without committing such howling gaffes. I will continue to speak up – it turns out I cannot help it – but I will be careful not to be glib about how robotic politicians can sound. After all, they are only trying to avoid being hounded by the media while they are meant to be marvelling at sparrows.

We have come a long way from the days of the Profumo affair and the scandals about politicians' personal lives. As a nation, we no longer expect gay politicians to pretend to have husbands or wives. When the Tory minister John Whittingdale seemed to be dating an S&M escort, there were merely some raised eyebrows and a smattering of laboured whip puns. (Geddit? Like the whip in Parliament?) By and large the public likes a bit of gossip but is fully signed up to the fact that if it doesn't affect your job, it is not a problem. Thirty years ago, the idea that the Prime Minister might have stuck his genitals into a pig, or that the Chancellor had been photographed with lines of coke, would have spelled the end of a career. When Piggate broke, I was in Kenya on a trip to see how the UK's international development funding was being spent. There is nothing like small talk about your prime minister's possible porcine deviances to get a meeting with Kenyan government officials and NGO bosses swinging. I was not particularly proud to be representing my country on that particular trip. Cheers, Dave.

What people don't like is if you lie about your life. If ever there was an example of where the truth is the best option, it is this. If you moralise about adultery, or don't vote for gay marriage because of the effect it will have on the Church, try not to get caught with your pants down sexting a woman who is not your wife. Also, just for the record, I have never met a woman who wanted to be sent a picture of a man's penis for the purposes of arousal. I know there may be some out there, but as a rule of thumb, if you are an MP – or anyone famous at all, in fact – if someone asks for a picture of your penis, assume they are a journalist.

It is very easy to imagine that you are not suited for a profession for all sorts of reasons. Women are often guilty of thinking of ten reasons why they can't do something before they think of a single reason why they can. The fear people have about their past, or even elements of their present, can crush their ambitions. We have it drummed into us when we are kids: 'If you do something illegal, it will be on your record for life.' The most common response you hear if you tell someone they should stand for Parliament is 'Oh I couldn't do that, too many skeletons in the cupboard.' It is clear that while we have come a long way from whispering about Ted Heath not having a wife, there is still some standard in public life that expects us to be saints instead of humans.

When you step up and put yourself forward for selection as a Labour candidate, you have an interview, usually with members of the regional and local party. They ask you a series of questions of their choosing, and then there is the standard equality stuff you have to go through in all interviews these days. Mind you, looking around at some politicians in the UK, I can't imagine how they answered the equality questions. Perhaps they lied. The final question you are asked in the selection process before you can pass go is 'Is there anything in your background that could damage the reputation of the Labour Party?' When I was asked this question, I sheepishly said, 'Well, I was a bit of a wild teenager.' The panel tittered in mild amusement. 'No criminal record, though? You've never harboured a criminal, started a coup?' 'Er, no, not as far as I can remember. I have had some strange lodgers, one man who read the *Sunday Sport*, but I don't think he was on the run from anything.'

I've known potentially brilliant people, real humans who have made mistakes in their lives, be put off stepping forward. So often we think that something we have done or are associated with in our past rules us out, or that the role we have cast ourselves in as carer, mother or just woman means that certain jobs or life experiences are not for us. Hands up all those who have said, 'I could never do that, what would my kids/partner/parents think?' or 'How would they cope?' You can all put your hands down now.

Most political parties will do a full-on scare exercise after you are selected. You are warned that the press will dig over every detail, every photo on Facebook. They will befriend your nan, turn up at your family funerals. Your family's life is no longer their own. They are conscripts; they go with you in this. You are told to talk to your family and friends to make sure they are OK with the intrusion, tell them about the risks. Your friends can no longer take pictures of you at social events. My friends are really good about it; they ask when it is all right to post and when it isn't. Mind you, group selfies of a load of thirty-something women dancing to Fuse ODG is hardly salacious. Luckily I don't hang out with the kind of people who think it is top lols to wear Nazi uniforms. Phew!

There was a time when I thought my brother's drug addiction and other things from my childhood would stop me being an MP. There was a terrible incident when I had already been selected as the candidate for Birmingham Yardley and Luke suffered a severe bout of drug-induced psychosis. My dad called me in despair, saying Luke was roaming the streets, so I set about trying to find him. I managed to track him down and drove to pick him up so I could take him to a mental health crisis facility. I found him on the streets of my prospective constituency in a complete state, violent, angry, scared and kicking off. As I was trying to get him into my car, he was shouting and attacking me. He leapt out of the car twice before I managed to actually calm him down. This all took place on the busiest road in my constituency during morning rush hour. I think it is safe to say that the political advisers of the world would agree that in media terms this does not look good.

On that day I nearly threw in the towel. I rang Caroline, my friend and political Svengali, and said I had to give up. I couldn't bear for my family to have to face publicity about Luke because of my decision to be an MP. Like always, she talked me round, told me what to do and how to compartmentalise the different areas of my life. On that day I decided I would always try to be honest about things. I signed up to the philosophy that if people want politicians to have real lives, experience the same woes as their constituents, actually speak from experience, then sometimes that looks ugly, frightening and desperate.

Before I was an MP, I was a councillor on Birmingham City Council. Shortly after I was elected, a colleague pulled me to one side to have a quiet and concerned word. He had been at an event launch for a local substance-misuse rehabilitation service at which my brother had stood up and told his story of recovery. At the beginning of his speech he had proudly declared to the assembled dignitaries that his little sister was a big cheese on the council. My colleague had wanted to warn me that this had happened. At first I thought he was saying it to break the news to me that my brother had been addicted to heroin and crack, as if I hadn't known. In fact he was worried that people might think badly of me in the future or try to use it against me. A sort of 'just to let you know, the cat's out of the bag'.

My brother is not junky scum, a useless waste of space or a feckless fool. He is poorly. I don't want to take away his personal responsibility for the pain he has caused me, my mom and dad, his partner, his son and our family. If you have never lived with a drug addict, you might not know the crushing humiliation of buying back your stolen belongings from the local Cash Converters. You might not be familiar with the constant guilt-tripping about his addiction being your fault. This was my life for many years before I was an MP, and for some since. Trying to hide it will not work, and it would be dishonest and stupid.

My experiences are not unique. Everyone I know has something dark in their lives or in their family history. Most people have made some howling mistake: cheated on their partner, lost touch with their parents or their children, devastated their friends, let people down or told lies. None of us are perfect. I don't believe in 'whatever doesn't kill you makes you stronger', but I do know that the shitty things in my life, the trials I have faced and the mistakes I have made, have made me a far more interesting and empathetic person. Frequently in Parliament I want to shout, 'If you had seen some of the things I have seen, you would never say what you just said.' We might not choose some of our painful moments; if we had our time again we might do it differently, but we don't have that privilege. My advice is never waste a crisis, press on the bruises and use the delicious pain to make you interesting and informed. Our lives are full to the brim of stuff we wish we hadn't done and people we really wish we could forget. It shouldn't control our futures; it should only enhance them.

So I'm a fan of seeing people's humanity. I find that those in Parliament who come across best with the public are those who are the truest reflections of themselves. I might not agree with the likes of Jacob Rees-Mogg on policy, but he is no identikit politician; he is always completely authentic. Nicholas Soames, Churchill's grandson, is hardly a rabble-rousing feminist; he's jolly well an old-school chap, but I like him because he doesn't ever try to hide it.

There is, however, a difference between speaking your mind and saying things that you think 'the common man' wants you to say. There is a real trend in politics at the moment to affect saying the unsayable to prove you are on a level with the general public. It is the equivalent of the contestant on *Big Brother* who declares, 'I say what I like, I'll tell you to your face, right, I've got to be true to myself.' And then proceeds to go around being a massive prick in the false name of truth. Being vile to everyone is not the same as being truthful or genuine; it is just being vile.

In Parliament there is a core group of fake truth speakers who call people like me a feminist zealot and regard diversity as codswallop. They think saying things like 'Why is it not acceptable to black up any more?' makes them the champions of those who boldly speak up. It is fairly alarming how these fake truth speakers have now found a home in the mainstream of politics. People like Donald Trump and Nigel Farage have noticed the anti-Establishment feeling and have clung on to it for dear life. The political rhetoric of the day has no room for truth, facts or experts; today we live in the era of entitled white rich blokes who claim to be sticking it to the man.

The modern world is full of charlatan soothsayers who use the idea of 'the Establishment' to frighten people into believing in them. The European Union referendum that took place in the UK was basically a battle fought on the lines of the people versus the Establishment. Trump in America is exactly the same. It is not what is being said – the facts, the policies – that matters; it is the idea that one side is the Establishment (Remain in the EU and Hillary Clinton in the States) and the other is the bold-as-brass,will-say-absolutely-anything-to-show-how-like-you-they-are (Brexit and Donald Trump). I want to be perceived as human, one of the people. That is what gives me the bravery to speak up. But I do not think that fronting lies simply by being willing to say anything shows humanity at all. It is the opposite of authentic. The likes of Nigel Farage and Boris Johnson and Donald Trump are nothing like anyone I have ever met down the pub, thankfully. Their authenticity is focus-grouped.

There were many things that annoyed me about the EU referendum. I think both sides were insulting, lacklustre and misjudged. Why anyone bothered to wave around big numbers or pound signs was a mystery to me. This debate was about culture, hearts and minds. The argument that bothered me most, though, was the idea that as a passionate Remainer I was part of the Establishment. The hard left of my party (with their posh London homes and privately educated children) say it of me as well, when they want to discredit me. If the people in my constituency living on the minimum wage believe that that's the case, I'll wear it. But no, during the EU referendum, it was Messrs Johnson and Farage who were saying it. Are you fricking kidding me?

During the campaign, I visited Hastings on the south coast with Jacob Rees-Mogg and a crew from Channel

4 news. We were there to discuss the referendum. The reason Channel 4 choose to put us on the telly together is partly because we get on, but the real interest lies in the juxtaposition between us. Two people with the same job from worlds so far apart that humour ensues. Can you guess which one is the Establishment figure? Me, the slightly sweary Brummie woman, or Jacob, the Old Etonian son of a lord? His Wikipedia entry literally calls him 'a member of an established Somerset family of coal mine owners'. I'm not criticising him for his background; he can no more help it than I can mine. He doesn't hide from it, which is part of his immense charm. But let's be honest, he is literally from establishments that wouldn't let me cross the threshold. There are clubs up and down the land that he could waltz into that I could only storm as an angry protestor. Luckily I don't like golf or clubs that have a door policy that doesn't allow you to wear Converse.

In Hastings, one particularly eager Brexiteer stood in front of me and Jacob and told us that remaining in the EU was a fat-cat stitch-up of big business. The fact that she began her argument with a story about her time as an expat (or, as I call them, migrants) sent for schooling in Hong Kong did little to help her case. It was laughable that she looked at me and Jacob and thought he was the one defending our great nation from such a fate, and that I was a fat-cat patsy. A little look at our employment history – Jacob a capital (fancy word for wealth) manager, me a charity worker – speaks to a different reality. Jacob would never have made this argument to me himself; he's much cleverer, kinder and more liberated than that. I'm fine with the differences between us, as is the Mogg himself, but we are aware of them at least.

The idea that remaining in the EU was an Establishment stitch-up or some sort of relinquishing of our democracy was a common argument heard during the campaign. But it was being put forward by a load of established figures, some of whom have family members in the House of Lords, making their argument that we the people needed to claw back our democratic power because we hadn't elected those rule-makers in Brussels a funny one. I'll look forward to Boris and Nigel joining me to fight for the reform of the House of Lords. Get the paint out, lads, we've got some placards to draw up. I'm going for 'Democracy isn't something we should get from Daddy Darling'. No, I thought not.

It seems that the electorate want people who look like them, MPs who appear human. They say to us, 'Please be real, feel like a human does and show it.' And then they feast on our humanity. If people really do want humans in Parliament, they must accept that we are just that. We are not perfect.

How do we stop the slide into becoming less human? I doubt I will go there willingly or quietly, but I fear I will get closer to it every day. Because when you say what you actually think and believe, it really hurts when it's dismissed, dissected and ridiculed. Don't get me wrong. I court the attention. I like my platform. No one cries for the tired, upset MP. I could have kept my head down. I could have stopped fighting back. Revelling in being a smart-arse ticks people off . . . Shocker! But sooner or later, the fear will take over. So you stop saying what you think, and start saying what you think people want to hear, or what they want you to say.

We've all got to ask ourselves the question: deep down do we really want our bosses, our leaders, our politicians to be human? If the answer is yes, then maybe we should let them try, and not leap about in delight when they cock it up from time to time. Imagine if every conversation you had with your mates was secretly filmed: do you not think you might phrase things wrong, or not come across as you actually are? Yes, politicians should not buy duck houses on the public purse; yes, they shouldn't sell their influence to foreign baddies. Hate the ones who do that if you like, but don't seek out reasons to hate us all as a homogenous group. After the revelations in the papers about Keith Vaz buying young men for sex came to light, more than one person said to me, 'You're all just a bunch of paedophiles, you MPs.' Yes that's me, well-known developer of services for children who have been sexually abused; of course the second I was elected I became a pervert.

The hatred of our politicians and the belief in a homogenous morality is what breeds the populist claptrap of the plastic everyman. It is directly to blame for the rise of UKIP, or Marine Le Pen. The same sense of false outrage has led people to believe that Jeremy Corbyn is the new messiah, just because he owns a bike and a tracksuit. If we continue to join in with the rhetoric that politicians and bosses and company directors are the baddies, we only have ourselves to blame when someone like Donald Trump becomes the leader of the free world. Most politicians, most people, in fact, are good and honest, just like Jo Cox. It is a shame we only see that when they are gone.

THE TRUTH ABOUT
TROLLING

Warning! The images and content you are about to see may cause some distress. If you are offended by bad language or graphic descriptions, you may want to look away now.

These are the words that should appear on my phone, iPad and inbox every morning. I want to give you, dear reader, the option to look away now, because I am about to talk about the very first time that I realised Internet trolling and abuse was a thing. In the words of the great Will Smith, here is a story all about how my life got flipped, turned upside down.

It was about 11.30 p.m. the night before my younger son's seventh birthday. As usual I had left present purchasing and wrapping until the last minute. I was sitting on the floor of my living room surrounded by parcels from Internet delivery sites, Mario Bros shiny wrapping paper, the arse ends of about four rolls of sellotape and a pair of nail scissors. Noticing that one of the presents I had ordered was not amongst the loot, I picked up my iPad to check my order confirmation emails. The first email in my inbox appeared in the viewing pane. It was from a man called Declan, and it read:

Hi, saw the case regarding what occurred in the Houses of Parliament.

Read up on it on several forums and I've seen some fairly disgusting things said against you.

I've attached a screenshot of some examples that were retrieved from this thread:

> ▲ [–] Fourteen_Words -3 points (+3|-6) 3 hours ago
> ▼
> He should have asked her to kindly shut the fuck up or he'd rape her in front of everyone.
>
> permalink

> ▲ [–] kakos_anthropes -3 points (+0|-3) 1 hour ago
> ▼
> You know what would be funny. Pouring molten iron down this cunt's cunt until she starts vomiting bullets. There are the kind of people who deserve to be bound up in a basement and repeatedly raped. I think watching her spirit die as you slowly removed strips of skin would be a really rewarding experience. Remove the eyes last, she should have her mutilated broken body by the last thing she sees.
>
> permalink

I'd obviously read about Internet trolling in the past. I was aware of the rape and death threats that had befallen my colleague Stella Creasy, the MP for Walthamstow, and the feminist campaigner Caroline Criado-Perez when they dared to demand that women should be represented on banknotes. Looking back, I suppose part of me should have expected to receive similar treatment as a woman who speaks up. I'm sad to say that now I do expect it, but then, in the warmth and safety of my family home, the sudden brutality of the imagery about my rape and mutilation was utterly shocking. But I didn't feel scared, I didn't feel that there was even the slightest chance that whoever kakos_anthrope was, he (or possibly even she) was ever going to hurt me.

I read the message out to my husband, who, as a veteran of the online gaming community, was thankfully immune to some of the brutal language used. He assured me it was just some lonely fool in his parents' basement desperate to shock. He suggested I send it to the police and pay it no more mind. Had anyone been a fly on the wall in my living room that night, I think they might have been shocked how calm our initial reaction was.

I carried on wrapping presents and my husband went off to the kitchen to make me a cuppa. Just after midnight, I fired the email over to Stella Creasy and asked her what I should do about it. She responded immediately with a series of instructions about making referrals to stalking services and speaking to the police and the Serjeant at Arms (responsible for security at the House of Commons).

Suddenly struck by the fact that a conversation about managing rape threats was occurring in the middle of the night between two women who had fought against the odds to get themselves to Parliament and used their position to speak up for women everywhere, I burst into inconsolable tears.

My husband reappeared, tea in hand, shocked by my transformation from calm to hysterical in a matter of minutes. Through my sobs I explained that I didn't think this stupid fool was going to hurt me; I was just sick and angry about how acceptable it still was to hate women. I felt so tired, so defeated. I thought about the efforts of the millions of other women who had given their lives, their souls, so that women like me could have an equal voice. I felt grief for my dead mother's efforts throughout the sixties, seventies and eighties. It felt as if she had wasted her time; that women who spoke up, women who achieved would always be hated, threatened and attacked. I felt completely and utterly devastated.

In the midst of my fit of despair, I thought of all of the women I had worked with who had been raped. I thought of all the times I had advised women to go to the police and tell them what had happened, even though I knew deep down that most likely they would never get justice. (I have seen many, many more victims be told that their perpetrator will face no further action than I have seen victims who got their day in court and a conviction to match their pain.) I thought of all the advice I had given out over the years about how we had to keep speaking up, keep telling our story even when it seemed hopeless. So I picked up my iPad, took a screen shot of what had been said about me and posted it on Twitter. I decided that even if this battle was going to be for nothing, I wanted to be a warrior not a forgotten civilian.

The reason I had received this abuse was because of events in Parliament the previous week, when I had laughed during a session of the Back Bench Business Committee. The Back Bench Business Committee is a committee of MPs that gets to decide which debates should be given time in the House of Commons. It is a bit like *Dragons' Den* for MPs: members come and ask if they can have debates on things ranging from peace talks in the Middle East to protecting ancient trees. On this particular day, Philip Davies MP said he wanted to hold a debate on International Men's Day and added that he didn't feel that men had enough opportunities to speak up in Parliament. I had absolutely no problem with the debate being held, but I did have a problem with the idea that men are somehow marginalised at Westminster. It is laughable. I commented that to me it seemed like every day was International Men's Day in Parliament. Bear in mind that I am the only woman on the Back Bench Business Committee of nine MPs. The make-up of the committee alone should have made him feel silly about his statement.

Because I am a woman with a voice that cuts through, because I am a woman who uses that voice at times to make feminist statements, apparently I deserve to be mutilated and raped. And this in 2016. Another email I received at the time read, 'I hope your sons end up hanging from a tree because of suicide. But even then you wouldn't be sad, because they are male.' I've never hurt anyone, I pay my taxes, support charities, help out in my local community and bake cakes for school fairs. I try to be a decent sort, but no matter what I do, the fact that I am a woman with an opinion is apparently worthy of a death sentence for both me and my children.

Warning! The text you are about to read contains descriptions of male privilege. Readers may be appalled by the level of stupidity taking place on the computers and media devices that can be found in the modern home. Those who think sexism is dead and wish to continue to live in that blissful ignorance should look away now.

The Back Bench Business Committee episode has led me to be the favourite target of the online world's men's rights activists. As best as I can tell, this particular group of people do absolutely naff all to help with men's issues such as suicide, prostate cancer or paternity leave. What they do very well is make all decent-minded people wonder if they should have the right to use the Internet or own pets. God forbid that they should start campaign groups or set up organisations; they have decided that the way to fight for men's rights is to make memes of me and women like me bound and gagged. Move over the civil rights movement: Martin Luther King Jr, you got nothing on these meme masters. If only the suffragettes, Gandhi or Aung San Suu Kyi had thought of mocking up karaoke videos about people they didn't like, the rights they struggled for would have been achieved in a jiffy. These men are not seeking men's rights; they just hate women and they hate them hard.

When you have five minutes, pop my name into the search bar on YouTube; the titles that appear really are a delight: 'Jess Phillips Wants To Be Raped! Extra special dose of mental retardation today!', 'Jess Phillips sucks – Feminist British MP', 'A Feminist Horror Movie', 'Jess Phillips Rapes Herself'. The crazy thing about this trend is that some of these men make their sole income from money accumulated by Internet clicks on YouTube. Apparently, I make good click bait. So there are men on the Internet who feed their families out of the spoils they get from abusing me.

At the time I exploded on to the men's rights activist scene, I was nominated for the Toxic Feminist of the Month award. A prestigious gong, I'm sure you will all agree, awarded by a political party called Justice for Men & Boys (and the women who love them). Check out their website: it features articles written only by the most choice commentators, with titles such as '13 reasons women lie about being raped' (incidentally, each of the reasons given is laughably stupid and easily disproved, my favourite being number 5: 'Women lie about rape if the sex is bad.' Wow! I think we can all agree that if that was the case, rape reporting would be going through the roof!). The leader of this group sent me a message on Twitter telling me of my nomination for the award, so I retweeted it, seeking votes in order to win said accolade.

I wanted to be in the honoured company of women such as Caroline Criado-Perez; Alison Saunders, the Director of Public Prosecutions; Vera Baird QC, the Police and Crime Commissioner; and Dame Sally Davies, the Chief Medical Officer for England. There are also Whiny Feminist and Gormless Feminist categories. I think Toxic is the best one; Toxic means we have power.

I'm delighted to report that I was that month's winner, and I'm hoping for best in show. The group's leader seemed to take umbrage at how pleased I was to have been nominated, and followed his tweet with a post on the website stating, 'I sent a tweet to Jess Phillips MP about her Toxic Feminist of the Month award, and she's now seeking votes. Confirmation of both her narcissism and stupidity.' Seems I touched a nerve. Perhaps it's because I got more votes on one street when I stood for election to Parliament than his political party managed in the whole country. Diddums.

The crux of why these people hate me is because I have a voice, and people listen to it. A woman with power is intolerable to them. The male rights activists of the world blame women like me for their failed dreams and their insignificance. They don't see that they were managing to be really rubbish before we came along, and the reason that their voice is insignificant is because they use it to say really dumb things. In the below-the-line comments section of every newspaper article written about me online, they spew vitriol about my body, about how I hate men, about how thick I am.

None of the videos, the below-the-line abuse, the vile tweets and fake accounts set up on Twitter in my name are, contrary to how they are presented, intended to be mean or to make me feel sad. Oh no! Every single word is designed to discredit and silence my voice. It is the silencing of women that is the sinister element in this, not the dumbass things that these men say.

I spend much of my spare time travelling around the country trying to encourage people to get involved in politics. I fight campaigns to secure better representation of women in Parliament, on local councils, within political parties and in the commentariat. I want women's voices to be heard. I am often contacted by young women who are looking for support and advice about how to deal with the vitriol, sexism and misogyny they face every time they speak. Most of these women tell me they're going to stop posting blogs and tweeting about their politics and their views. The very first thing I say to every one of them is 'Don't stop, whatever you do. Don't let them silence you.'

Very specific tactics are used by trolls to silence people on the Internet; these are dog piling and isolating. Dog piling is when hundreds – or thousands in my case – of people send you messages over a short space of time. The worst case of this happening to me was when one of the most prolific men's rights dunderheads made a comment about how he wouldn't even rape me. Yes, in the twenty-first century we live in a world where saying you won't rape someone is a thing. Apparently I'm not good enough for raping, because raping is what we do to the pretty women, and I bet they are thrilled! On the face of it, this might appear ridiculous and a juvenile thing to say, sort of like when my kids try to excuse saying insulting things by chirping, 'Gotcha! I didn't mean it, it's opposites day.' However, it is actually an ingenious way for these oversized delinquents to talk about me and rape in the same sentence without breaking the law. It is against the law to threaten to rape someone; it is not against the law to say you *wouldn't* rape someone. I don't know about you, but trying to get around the law on rape threats is not something I normally trouble myself with.

As soon as the initial degenerate had made this comment, along came all his Bebop-and-Rocksteady-style duffel bag carriers to join in. A twat-signal was beamed across the ether and thousands of messages about the different ways people from all over the world would not rape me poured in. The tweets were coming thick and fast. When this happens, the feeling is akin to being stood in front of an enormous angry mob waving burning torches and pitchforks. A glance at my Twitter feed that day was a bit like reading a really sinister Dr Seuss:

> I will not rape her on a plane
> I will not rape her on a train
> I will not rape her in the car
> I will not rape her on a star
> I will not rape her HERE OR THERE
> I will not rape her anywhere

I will not rape her on a tram
I will not rape her, MAN-I-AM

People often say to me, 'Just block them and forget about them.' The trouble is that with so many messages coming in at once, you couldn't possibly block them all unless you employed teams of people to do it for you. From the time a dog-piling attack begins until it finishes you cannot use social media because you are drowned out. It stops you from being able to communicate with anyone else and makes it impossible for people to contact you, because you cannot see them amongst all the rape chatter. For the time being you are silenced. Eventually the storm dies down and only the last straggler is still going, sad that they missed the fun because they were on holiday in Nowheresville.

In the dying breaths of a dog pile, people revert to sending you emails, clogging up your inbox with their newly elaborate messages, no longer confined to 140 characters. This is even more damaging, as my email is the place where my constituents talk to me. If I can't bear to look at my emails, I am also not seeing the messages from parents of autistic kids without school places, or council house residents who've had no hot water for days. It is when this happens that being a feminist is detrimental to my job. When your identity becomes a barrier to your performance, there is a very serious problem. After one of these storms, people think I just carry on as I did before, except it is not exactly as before because I am now mindful of stopping it happening again. Bang! They have silenced me.

The dog-piling technique is straight out of the playbook of domestic abusers. It is coercive control. It drills the same messages into you over and over again and isolates you from other voices. If this technique doesn't work, the savvier Internet troll will ramp up to Plan B: isolation. This consists of abusing other people who talk to you in the hope that it will put them off doing so. This happens to people who talk to me every single day, and it bothers me more than anything else. I frequently have to apologise to people who have mentioned me on Twitter or Facebook for the abuse that then gets hurled at them. Every time I do anything that someone wants to publicise, I have to warn them that being associated with me means I'm likely to poison their comments. This is not a shock to journalists who interview me, especially the female ones; they know the drill. It's less pleasant for the church in my constituency who have invited me to a fun day, or the local school who want me to come to their parents' coffee morning.

When I agreed to write this book, in my initial meeting with my editor, Jocasta, we talked about plans for publicity and I had to say, 'You do realise that any publicity will come with a whole load of abuse.' I am tough enough to deal with this stuff, but I think it is only right to give fair warning to those around me who might not be. The hilarious thing about the people who carry out this kind of isolation and Internet bullying is that they are often the same people who bang on about free speech. They think they should be allowed to say anything! What they mean of course is free speech for people who look and sound like them. The Internet is full of little Donald Trumps building Mexican walls around those they don't like in the name of righteousness and freedom of speech.

I'm ashamed to say that this isolation technique is mostly used not by the men's rights types, who prefer the bukake nature of a dog pile, but people within my own political party. During 2015 and 2016, the Labour Party spent most of its time in long-drawn-out and divisive leadership elections. This meant that its presence online was mostly a war of attrition. I imagine a similar story could be told about the US primaries and the subsequent presidential election. I did not support the leadership bid of Jeremy Corbyn in either of the two contests we have had in as many years. This meant that I have been subject to streams and streams of abuse. I have been called a traitor, a scab, a neoliberal Zionist puppet of America. If people talk to me or about me on Twitter or in the newspaper, hundreds of angry banner wavers will shout them down.

During the 2015 leadership campaign, I supported Yvette Cooper. Politics is a rough old game and there is a certain expectation of being hated that comes with the territory. It is not politicians being attacked that bothers me so much. It's more the fact that women are being kept quiet on the Internet. Even worse than the violent, threatening and blatant misogyny is the 'shut up' bit. Because it is working. Women are shutting up. Not because they are scared, not because they believe the threats, but because it is so tiring that whenever you speak, you face hatred due to the make-up of your chromosomes or your political opinions. Lots of young women told me that they had stopped retweeting or posting articles about Yvette because it meant that they got grief for the rest of the day. I'm sure the same thing happened to supporters of every leadership camp. I only experienced it from people supporting Corbyn, but I know it happens across the board.

The worst element of this silencing technique was the attempts to discredit me in order that my voice would no longer be worth listening to. Of course, this is all part of the political game, but usually it is your opponents who do it, not your own side. In 2016 there were two occasions when the discrediting and bullying from my own party spilled off the Internet and into my real life. This is when you realise that the online stuff is not a joke.

The first time it was done by a woman I actually know, a woman who is a friend of my best friend. With hindsight, she has all the hallmarks of the kind of person who would troll me about the Labour Party. As best as I can tell, she is an armchair activist, a warrior on social media. Out of nowhere she sent me some smug Corbyn rally picture, specifically copying me in to the tweet to have a pop at me. I can see no reason for her to send this other than to be divisive. From my perspective she was basically shrieking, 'I'm right about the Labour Party, you're wrong, nah nah na na nah.'

Now I want to interrupt this tale for an educational

interlude on how not to behave on Twitter. If you are going to clutch your pearls about getting a cutting response from me, can I politely suggest that you don't copy me in to your bile in the first place. Don't talk about me and tag me in the comment and then get all outraged if I respond. If you want to have a discussion, no problem. I pride myself on being responsive to real debate online, even when I disagree with your views. Just a little tip, this is not how you start a discussion:

Hey, look how great and right I am about everything . . . yay me, I'm totes right, unlike @jessphillips. #jezwecan

If you want a discussion, I suggest:

Hi @jessphillips, I don't agree with you on X issue, I think Y, any thoughts?

Or alternatively, if you just want to slag me off so you and your blinkered 'we are so right about everything' mates can jerk off over it, here's my suggestion:

Hey, look how great I am about everything . . . yay me, I'm totes right, unlike Jess Phillips. #jezwecan

The removal of the @ sign means you have just had an opinion. Having an opinion and loathing me are perfectly acceptable. Knock yourself out. You have essentially slagged someone off behind their back, and let's face it, who hasn't done that? If you tag me in the comment, you're just being a massive douche who in the offline (real) world is the kind of coward who runs over and calls you a name and then runs off again.

Anyway, back to the story, in which said tweeter had not followed the aforementioned advice and was an aforementioned name-calling douche. I responded, perhaps foolishly, with a comment about how mass rallies obsessed with an individual would do nothing for the people in my constituency suffering the bedroom tax. She then accused *me* of being a troll. I pointed out that it was not me who came out from under the bridge gritting my teeth, it was her. I was in fact on holiday with my lovely family and lots of our lovely friends. I was not tweeting about politics, I was not inciting any attention, I was mainly eating baguettes and playing weird avant-garde lawn games. She need not have copied me in.

When she accused me of being a troll she wrote, 'Nonsensical and profoundly desperate trolling from an MP who can't and won't grasp democracy in action.' She copied in a rabble-rousing left-wing journalist as well, in the hope, I assume, that he would follow suit and join in the attack. He didn't. She talked about me as a thing, a job role, a totally faceless nothing, rather than a woman whose children she had played with or a person who had lent her my van so she could move office. She didn't think of our mutual friend having to see her slagging me off and how she might feel. The same friend who worries about me all the time because of the vitriol I face, more so than nearly anyone in my life. The woman who texts me saying, 'Just wanted to check in and make sure you're OK, I've seen the hideousness online.'

I thought about responding with 'Look at this sad (insert job title) who knows nothing about courtesy or reality and is a massive cliché.' But I didn't because I know it would have been a hurtful thing to do, and to be so public about it would have been humiliating for her. Also some of the people who regularly wade in to defend me when fools attack have millions of followers, so me using the same tactic of public shaming and dehumanising would have been worse for her and would have prolonged the whole episode. Contrary to her assertions, I try not to act like an Internet troll. I wanted the whole thing to stop because, if I am being completely honest, it really upset me. Not because I give a toss what she thinks; not even because I'd already had to make sure our mutual friend was OK and not worrying. I was upset because I have become such fair game on the Internet that people I bump into in the street, have colleagues in common with, might have to share a wedding toast or two with over the years, think that trying to upset me is sport. I'm nothing more to these people than a target for hatred; even people I've carried home in a cab drunk don't seem to remember that I am a person.

The second time Internet vitriol from my own party spread its nasty little wings down from the cloud and into my living room was thanks to a left-wing website seemingly set up entirely to support Jeremy Corbyn's leadership bid but dressing itself up as an unbiased and independent truth-speaking medium. At least the *Daily Mail* knows it is a rabid conservative mouthpiece.

On 15 September 2016, the Conservative government released a statement detailing how they intended to U-turn on housing benefit caps for women in refuges and promised to create a future model for sustainable funding. This was something that I had campaigned on for months and months. Every time I got the opportunity to raise my voice on the issue I did. I posed public questions directly to the Prime Minister, begging him to support refuges. I called for and took part in many debates, putting pressure on the government week in, week out. I worked with national and local charities across the country to write letters, sign petitions, tell their stories. I went on the telly, on the radio and I wrote articles. Along with others I screamed and shouted. I used my voice to fight for people without a voice. I had meeting after meeting with government MPs and lobbied people I thought could help me swing it. When the government listened, I was elated. What they offered was not perfect, but it was a damn sight better than what we'd had before. On that day, being an MP mattered, all the hours spent away from my family, from my own bed, all the crap that I had to put up with was worth it because I was part of a team that had helped change something.

There has not been a day in Parliament when I have not fought hard for victims of domestic violence. One of my colleagues commented recently that since I have been in Westminster, the profile of violence against women has been elevated beyond recognition. We are not meant to blow our own trumpets, I know that, but sod it, I'm really proud of what I've done. I got people's voices heard, people who on their own would never have had a chance. This was an example of the Labour Party doing a good thing. In the long summer of attrition that preceded this day, proud moments were few and far between. It was worth being happy about.

But did the Labour Party leadership herald this success? Did they praise my work, and that of others involved? No they did not. Instead my name appeared on a list of those who had abused Jeremy Corbyn. Dubbed a 'purge list' by journalists, it appeared in most newspapers, which felt like an invitation for activists to come after me. It appeared to work.

Evolve (an ironic name, considering it clearly hasn't) is a website set up in August 2016 (funny that it started during the leadership contest) carrying only pro-Corbyn propaganda. Some wannabe revolutionary blog writer decided that this week of all weeks it was high time to discredit my record on domestic violence. This blogger called and emailed around women's refuges trying to reach my old boss, asking questions about whether I had ever really interacted with the women at the Women's Aid where I worked. They were trying to claim that since I was a business development manager there, I had never met the victims and therefore was faking the stories I told. As if local Women's Aids are huge organisations where staff are hived off in fancy business departments. I didn't have some swanky glass-walled corner office. I barely had space for my desk, which was normally surrounded by donated car seats, baby baths and toys. I suppose I can't expect them to have known this; the author of the blog is a twenty-two-year-old who spends most of her time online talking about Pokémon GO. She has probably never had a proper job and can afford to write spurious articles all day because Mummy and Daddy are paying her bills.

I wish these Internet lurkers realised that on this occasion discrediting and silencing my voice also silenced the voices I was trying to amplify – the vulnerable victims and their children. Even though my old boss refused to speak to Evolve, the article came out the following day and I spent the next twenty-four hours ignoring questions on Twitter and posts on Facebook from fools who said things like 'Had no idea Jess Phillips' position with women's charity was a business development manager. Nothing wrong with that, but her brand has been to sell herself as a practitioner/expert in the field. She had zero to do with the service provision.'

The funny thing was, the front-bench politician who did take to Twitter to thank me for my efforts was not from my own party; the Rt Hon. Damian Green, the Secretary of State for Work and Pensions, wrote, 'Happy to make this decision welcomed by @jessphillips. She ran a good campaign.' You couldn't make it up: the government minister who had to make the U-turn on his party's policy was more grateful than activists from my own side.

The people who spun this story were more interested in making me look bad, shutting me up for their own agenda, than they were in saving the lives of abused women and children. I really hope that these people, and the ones who leapt on the story, feverishly feasting on a chance to discredit me, will fight for the vulnerable if they manage to get rid of me. I hope they realise that you can't build refuges out of placards and promises.

I don't want to get all Mary Whitehouse about this. I love the Internet. It's full of brilliant people saying funny things that you wish you'd said (and will later pass off as if you had). My kids' minds are blown by the amazing things they see online every day. I just want to make sure that the brilliant stuff is from everyone. If we allow a tiny minority sitting at their computers in their pants to spew hatred at those of us paying the tampon tax, we will limit how wondrous it can be. We have to accept that the Internet is an alternative world that we walk around in, pin our interests to, somewhere we share our loves and woes. But unless you are willing to walk up to me or any woman in the street and say, 'God, you are so fat, I bet your husband is cheating on you and your kids hate you', don't do it online.

Under no circumstances do I want to be seen as a victim. I have worked with victims of sexual violence and I don't have a candle to hold to their experiences. I am determined not to behave like a victim online. This will be a shock to all those who love to make memes of me with the words 'playing the victim card' scrawled across my face. I think the best strategy for combating abuse is to call it out. I remain defiant in the face of the abuse I get. I realise this is not for everyone, and lots of people prefer just to block, report it and move on with their lives. These people are probably happier than me and they definitely waste considerably less time than I do. I just can't help myself, because I know I am cleverer than those who abuse me. Some of the best, funniest things I have ever written are the reposts to trolling on Twitter.

I found it incredibly amusing one week to just reply to all the trolls who contacted me with the video of Justin Bieber's 'Love Yourself' and the message 'My momma don't like you and she likes everyone.' Stella Creasy has a great strategy of pretending all the trolls are her mom and responding with sulky teenage-style reposts. Ruth Davidson, the leader of the Scottish Conservative Party, is a leader in the field, but the troll-slayer general is of course J. K. Rowling.

I know smart-arse comebacks are not for everyone, although I do encourage you to try, should you face a trolling. It can be incredibly good for the soul. The one thing I find really helps when I am suffering a crap storm of abuse online is counter-speech. Sometimes if I am going on the telly or about to do something I think will attract Internet hobgoblins, I put out a request for cat pics and kindness to flood my feed. I can cope with loads of vitriol and hatred when it is interspersed with pictures of people lying on the floor with a hamster on their face. If we can't stop the Internet grumps, we can use their own tactics to defeat them. Dog piling with love. We need to form a misogyny counter-speech army, sending encouraging messages or friendly pictures to anyone who is getting it rough. All the troll-slaying women I have mentioned do this for each other. We roll up our sleeves and wade in with loveliness, or funny gags. The women in the PLP are pretty good at employing this strategy when one of our number is in the firing line. Men are welcome in the squad too, and I'm happy to make up badges, or perhaps branded berets.

For all that I can be chippy about the trolls and can certainly put up a fight, the Internet makes me feel as if I'm wading through treacle. Every time I speak out about anything feminist, I am shot down by people calling me fat, common or stupid. I receive abuse all day, every day, especially on Twitter. Mostly I am tough and it doesn't bother me a bit. I'll be on the train, with my work done, and I'll turn on my phone and think, 'Right, I've got half an hour – amuse me!' But the truth is, it's been getting worse.

When I talk to my male colleagues about this stuff, they say that they do get it, but never ever as bad as the women. Before she died, Jo Cox co-wrote an article in the *Guardian* with our colleague Neil Coyle about how they had concerns over Jeremy Corbyn's leadership. Jo was horrendously trolled on Twitter by Corbyn supporters saying things like 'Look in the mirror Jo what do you see? I see a traitor looking at me' and 'Jo Cox and Neil Coyle sign their political death warrants. Tick tock, scabs.' These messages are incredibly chilling considering that the man who is accused of killing Jo claimed that she was a traitor. At the time of this abuse, Jo sent me a text saying she could do with some back-up, as the trolls were getting to her. The same day I saw Neil Coyle in the Commons chamber and made a beeline for him, asking if he was OK and whether he too needed any counter-speech support. He told me that he'd had one or two messages but nothing too bad. I know this is not a scientific test or anything, but it seemed to me and to the two MPs involved that Jo was the one taking the worst of the attacks, or at least she was the one feeling them.

How these sorts of comments are received by women is a really important part of the story. Unfortunately the sexist element of the trolling that I receive plays on all the insecurities I have always had about myself. They call me goofy or say my teeth are stained (which they are thanks to medicine I was given as a baby with pneumonia; look it up, it's an actual phenomenon). Trolls call women fat; mine like to obsess about my boob size and my ugly face. They will tell young women who live their lives on the Internet that they are stupid and common and ugly and dirty, all things that young women are telling themselves every day – and that is why it is so dangerous.

I wish there was something I could say to make this better. I could tell you that you are beautiful and badass and that is the reason they are trying to attack you, but I know how difficult that is to believe even if it is completely true. Ignoring the hatred, reporting it and blocking it is the quickest way to get rid of it. Leave the fighting-back to people like me if it is really upsetting; drop me a tweet if you like – I'll have your back. I think the best advice I can give is to identify a couple of people you can call on if online controversialists come after you. Internet trolls too stupid to know the law who threaten death and rape should be reported to the police straight away. Thanks to brave women who have kept on pushing in the past, these offenders are appearing more frequently in our courtrooms. In my head, my most frequent aggressor was some American figurehead; turned out he was a bloke from Swindon whose job seemed to entirely consist of being on the Internet. Imagine that every Internet troll is a bloke from Swindon who can't get a job, and you'll soon realise your own superiority.

The reason that this sort of thing is still worse for women today is because we live in a patriarchal society where many men want us just to be wives and mothers. They look at women like me and Jo, and they feel that women's liberation has taken something from them: women holding jobs and being economically empowered seems directly linked with their own dispossession. They think their situation is our fault – as though they could have had my job if I hadn't taken it. They will literally say that feminism is cancer.

Just as society and Parliament are male-dominated and patriarchal, so is the Internet. This is hugely problematic. Every time a woman who has faced this Internet mob goes to say anything, she pauses and thinks, have I got the energy or time to deal with this today? and then she puts down her phone. She is silenced when she might have had the wittiest, most insightful thing to say. It could have been ground-breaking. She could have been about to launch the campaign that would end poverty in Africa, or stop offshore tax-dodging skulduggery, or change the state of mental health services for all. She could have been frickin' amazing, but instead she stopped.

We have to try and make platforms for speaking out more female-friendly, because at the moment they aren't. We need to be looking at what comes next and creating new online environments, those with a wide reach but also where women feel safe. We women need to step up and use our commercial power. Mumsnet is a great example of a platform led by women and largely moderated by women, where this abuse and trolling simply doesn't fly. Those mums can get fiery at times, but never would a Dr Seuss-style rape marathon take place.

So what can we do to make sure women's voices are heard? Together with other amazing female parliamentarians and feminist and equality activists I have been involved in launching a Recl@im the Internet campaign. We are attempting to look at the laws and regulations that could be better used to stop abuse. This will not be easy, but the police do at least seem willing to join the conversation, even though it is essentially going to massively increase their workload. The campaign is working with tech companies like Google, Facebook and Twitter to create filters and use technical jiggery-pokery to filter abuse away.

My husband tells me that on some Internet gaming sites (I suspect this description makes me sound like a completely clueless and embarrassing mom) they make all the cheats and bullies play together. They basically ghettoise the baddies so that the more gentle gun-toting warriors can carry on with their within-the-rules fun. If only we could create a sort of online sin bin for the Internet bully bores so they could all just talk about how they wouldn't rape each other. I don't have the solution; I imagine the financial bottom line for companies like Twitter will be the thing that forces change. When women like me finally quit our Twitter habit because fighting abuse is just too exhausting, that will send the alert.

For now I would ask that we all keep up the conversation about improving the Internet experience for women and girls. The abusers rely on us throwing our hands in the air in horror and giving up because we believe the Internet is too hard to regulate. We have to keep talking about this, keep moaning, keeping reposting the abuse we get to highlight it. We have to do this so that all our voices can be heard, so that freedom of speech isn't drowned out by faceless avatars, and so that women can speak up in the face of lively debate and challenge, and not be silenced into submission.

The truth about trolling for me is simple. No matter how many times they call me thick, common or childish, the truth is I am none of those things and they know it. My voice gets heard and they can't stand it. They hate me because I am winning.

THE TRUTH ABOUT
SPEAKING THE TRUTH

My voice is deeper than I'd like. On the phone people frequently think I am a man and call me sir or think when I say Jess that I have said Jeff. My accent is the most derided brogue in the country and one of the rarest in Parliament. 'Ow you're from Biiiiirminggam,' people will sing-song terribly when mimicking it. According to the Flesch–Kincaid test (grading of readability), the speeches I make in Parliament are at a level that would be understood by the average 16–17-year-old. To summarise, my voice is apparently androgynous and stupid, and what I say is teenage. In spite of this, my voice is and always has been my greatest asset. It is the tool I use to build relationships, to comfort those in need and to show my love. It is the weapon I use to damn my opponents. It is no surprise then that it is the thing people fear the most, and for those who don't like me, it is my voice that must be discredited, ridiculed and belittled.

The age of Internet trolling has resulted in a frequent

and visceral objection to women's opinions, but the diminishing of our voices is not a new phenomenon. Recently I read Brian Lavery's book *The Headscarf Revolutionary*, about an amazing working-class woman called Lillian Bilocca. Big Lil, as she was known, rallied the women of Hessle Road in Hull to campaign for safety on British trawlers in the 1960s after the death of fifty-eight fishermen. They took their fight to Westminster and won. This woman and her sisters in arms were stone-cold heroes.

When Big Lil spoke up and sought publicity for her cause by appearing on an ITV chat show, a letter sent to the Hull *Daily Mail* declared: 'If anyone is to be interviewed on any future programme, let it be someone who is able to speak and express themselves properly.' She received anonymous letters too, proving that the egg-face Twitter trolls of modern times are not the first faceless cowards: 'Why don't the people of Hull kidnap you, tie some bricks around your neck and drop you in the Humber, you big fat greasy Maltese whore'; 'You are a fat common slob and do not know how to talk.'

The truth, of course, was that her ability to communicate made her dangerous to those who sought to silence her. So often when women's voices are shamed it is exactly because they are less exclusive and easier to understand. If a working-class woman can speak to people better than an Establishment man, the Establishment are in trouble.

The local secretary of the Trawler Officers' Guild stated, 'I have been asked by the wives of some of my members to state that the action of Mrs Bilocca has not enhanced the image the public may have of fishermen's wives. Women who have lost men have had the least to say, which is what we admire.' Fifty-eight people had died and this bloke admired silence! If fifty-eight people had been killed in my community, I would have screamed like a big old common banshee to anyone who would listen. It is sad to realise that fifty years on from the days of the headscarf revolutionaries, female voices are still so jarring to the established order.

So I ask everyone reading this book to speak up. We all suffer from impostor syndrome, thinking that someone else will always say something cleverer than us. That someone else is funnier, more insightful, that someone else will write a better book, make a better speech, do a better dance. No one can delegitimise our voices better than we can ourselves. I would ask you to tell your internal dialogue to politely do one. There are plenty of people eagerly waiting to silence you. There are hordes of reptilian self-styled libertarians poised to attack. Don't join in with them; after all, if you saw these tossers walking down the street with women-hating banners, you wouldn't march alongside them.

In March 2015, I travelled to the UN in New York at the invitation of the National Democratic Institute to speak at the launch of the #NotTheCost Call to Action. The event was hosted by Secretary of State Madeleine Albright to raise the issue of violence faced by women in politics. I felt a bit of a fraud sat amongst mayors, senators, and deputy presidents from Kosovo, Peru, Sri Lanka, Uganda and many more. Each woman stood up and talked about the violence they had faced in their political life. Stories of being held at gunpoint, threatened with kidnap. Stories of how women were expected to perform sexual favours in order to progress, damned if they didn't and shamed if they did. Undaunted, they all continued to speak up. It is dangerous to be a woman with a voice, but it is considerably more dangerous for us to shut up.

I tend to read books by women, find female speakers more inspiring. Women seem to be able to say in a few words what men say in hundreds. Perhaps the fact that I have a million things on my mind at any one moment means I don't have time for pomposity and language that excludes. Say what you mean and then bloody well get on with it. The world would be incredibly boring if we let all those people who allegedly know everything say everything. So much of politics – so much of everything – is dominated by men saying things. Don't be a sayer, be a doer.

Week in week out, people seek my advice about how to get a campaign off the ground, or come to me asking how to get people involved with their organisation, their company, their action. I have little advice other than just do it. In my local area I have hundreds of volunteers who turn up to help in my political campaigning. I have been asked to run training on how I built this capacity. Don't get me wrong, there are tricks to starting the conversations, drawing people in, but they are little more complicated than talking to people about what they care about rather than talking at them about what *you* care about. The crux of how I get people involved would amount to a training session of five seconds: I ring them up and I ask them to help. I don't worry about all the reasons why they might not want to, I don't worry about how embarrassed I'll be if they say no. I don't wait to be given orders or ask permission to take action. I don't ring Jeremey Corbyn's office and say, 'Do you mind awfully if I try to change this law?' There will always without fail in every meeting I go to be someone who says, 'Oh, you can't do that' or 'When I tried that it didn't work.' Smile at these people politely and just do whatever you want to do anyway. Be more Big Lil.

People make mistakes all the time. I certainly do. We all drop wild clangers. But I speak up regardless of the risk because I am considerably less important than the struggle. I don't intend to sound like a pious bore, more like your nan telling you to 'stop bleeding moaning and crack on'. I'd ask everyone reading this book to pen an email to your boss today and ask, 'Can you tell me how many women hold leadership positions in this organisation and how many men? Also, could I have a look at the mean wage of women in the organisation and the mean wage of men?' This does not make you a troublemaker. It is a simple question, and unless your employer has something to hide, it should be pretty easy to answer. If you get a disappointing answer, which you probably will, write back and ask how you can be part of the solution to change it.

Two of my mates worked at a small company lorded over by a small man who had slept with half his workforce and then promoted them out of fear of a sexual harassment case. He discriminated against one of my friends while she was pregnant and reduced her pay after she returned to work. When she came over to ask my advice about this discrimination, I said, 'You have to tell him in no uncertain terms that if he does not give you some sort of settlement, reinstate your wages and compensate you, you will take him to a tribunal, where either his wife will get to hear about his indiscretions or his staff will have to commit perjury.' My friend did not want to cause trouble for the other people at work; she immediately considered how it might affect her colleagues and the company. I had to gently remind her that it was not her fault her boss was a massive douche. It was his actions that had led to these consequences, not hers. I was astounded by how little power a man has to have before his staff and his peers are willing to turn a blind eye. I told my friend that her voice and the public airing it would get in a tribunal was mightier than any limp-wristed hold her boss had. Guess what? She did it, and she won. Her voice was heard, her case was answered. Our silence is complicity, our volume is napalm.

I had a meeting a year ago with Polly, the amazing boss of Women's Aid. We decided that we wanted to speak up on behalf of all of the women damaged by the family court system in the UK. Since legal aid has been so badly cut, many women who have been battered, raped and abused can no longer access legal representatives to help them. Every day a woman stands in a British court and defends herself against her domestic violence perpetrator who is trying to gain access to her children. Survivors find themselves being cross-examined by the perpetrator, or by the perpetrator's barrister. Imagine for a second what it would be like to be questioned in public by a man who has raped you. These women do this to protect their children from dangerous men. I've heard about cases of men released from prison for murder to spend a day in court seeking access to their children. Polly and I knew that if we took on this campaign we would face anger from the fathers' organisations, which claim that women are favoured by our courts. Just to be clear, 70 per cent of cases in family court have an element of domestic violence, and only 1 per cent of fathers are ever refused access. It is a myth that women are favoured. We knew that if we spoke up we risked men dressed as superheroes clambering on to our homes and our offices. We knew we would face a vitriolic backlash. We were right.

In the debate in the House of Commons on this subject, my colleague and friend Angela Smith spoke of the case of her constituent Claire Throssell. Claire's ex-husband had been granted access by the family courts to her sons Jack and Paul, aged twelve and nine, against Claire's wishes. Clare had suffered domestic abuse and had been controlled and coerced by her husband for decades. On one of his access visits, he lured Jack and Paul to the attic of their house and set the house on fire.

Both boys died from their injuries. You are damn right we are going to speak up about this issue. I don't care who scales the side of my house. At the end of her speech, Angela read out a tweet she had received while the debate was under way. It said, 'Man hating at its finest. Well done.' We had sat in the chamber for hours, telling heartbreaking stories of a failing system; never once was there even a tiny fraction of man hating. For those who wish to silence us, smearing us in this manner is the simplest way to discredit our well-researched and gut-wrenching words. I do not hate men; I hate men who kill their children.

Claire is one of the bravest women I know. She faces the horror of what happened to her and her children and still speaks up every single day. Every victim who dares to be brave and use their voice in a courtroom does it not to self-promote, but to protect themselves and their children, because nobody else is going to speak up for them. All those MPs, men and women, who spoke in the debate that day did it knowing full well the reaction we would get from people desperate to hold on to their misplaced power and privilege. Polly and I knew that speaking up would cause us grief, trolling, time-wasting arguments and possibly worse. Speaking up matters. I punch the air every time I see a woman doing it; I urge them on. When the journalist Cathy Newman spoke of her abortion when fighting against aggressive pro-life protesters; when Nimko Ali tours the country talking about her female genital mutilation; when the little girl in my son's class holds a piece of paper saying 'When I grow up I want to be prime minister': each and every time I cheer. You could be one of these brave women too, or you could be the person who encourages and helps them to be brave. I want to be cheering for you.

Don't believe it when people tell you no one will care what you say. If you want to write something, anything – it doesn't have to be about rights and justice; it could be a jam recipe or a love song – do it. During the writing of every chapter of this book my finger has hovered over the send button on the email to my editor in which I say, apologetically, 'I don't think this is any good.' The world is now a stage for all of us. Don't let YouTube be full of overweight men with beards rapping ditties about feminazi hoes. Crowd them out with your vlogs about something you have made, something you have done. Hell, talk about periods, horse riding or One Direction if you want to, I don't care. I just want your voice out there. Write a blog about your love of *Sweet Valley High* novels, ask to speak at your next staff meeting about a good idea you have had to improve annual leave allocation. Vocalise that sarcastic comment that comes into your head when your boss patronises you. Terrify yourself; it is never as bad as you thought it was going to be.

When I drive past an overweight woman going for a jog, I have to stop myself from rolling down the window and whooping at her public efforts. That woman looks strong and powerful to me. That woman screams, 'I don't give a toss if I don't look like Jessica Ennis, I'm doing this for me.' When my husband asks me why I don't go out running when I complain about being unfit, I reply, 'I couldn't do that, I'd look a fool, people would laugh at me.' I wish I could be the me in the car who thinks that woman is powerful. We all wish that we could be that kick-ass woman doing that kick-ass thing.

I hope that if nothing else, this book shows you that I am not exceptional, that I am worried and scared about using my voice. I hate it when people shout me down or call me thick, as they do every day. I always think there is someone better for the job than me. I'm just like you; you are kick-ass too, just like every woman.

ACKNOWLEDGEMENTS

So the first person I must thank is Laura from Tibor Jones. There would be no book without her. She bothered to stalk me for long enough to convince me to write it – forget the bravado, I never thought anyone would give a damn about what I had to say before she popped up in my inbox. I was painfully slow in dealing with her at times but her patience and skill got this book written.

To Jocasta Hamilton and all the team at Hutchinson for believing in me and helping me understand this world. Jocasta, you were a wise editor for steering me away from putting sexy vampires in the book. When I struggled with my own imposter syndrome Jocasta was always on hand to be my cheerleader.

I must thank Owen Bennett and Graeme Demianyk from the Huffington Post for being my original writing cheerleaders when I'd never written more than a postcard.

There are many of my friends I must thank. Without

Alex McCorkindale, Amy Eddy, Jayne Aziz, Jess Southwood and Ruth Wenban-Smith I would be nowhere near as sane as I am and could not have written this book. I want to thank Gemma Harvey and Amy Terry for being my rocks in the dark days of being a poorish, youngish mom; Caroline and Eleanor for teaching me many things but, for the purposes of this book, mainly that motherhood has sod-all to do with biology; and Matthew Hamilton and Adam Sach for teaching me that families are the people we choose, not just those we are given – for this I am thankful.

To Sara Ward and all at Sandwell Women's Aid, and all the women of Women's Aids across the UK. They taught me everything I know about violence. I've tried to portray their spirit in this book. It turns out that if you work somewhere that bangs on about empowering women every day, it sinks in.

To Amrita, Sophie, John, Ali and Matt and everyone in the Yardley Labour Family, thanks for your loyalty, love and hard work.

To the Women's Parliamentary Labour Party who have had their lives captured in this text. I hope I speak for many of you in some of my frustrated and euphoric moments. Special Thanks to Alison McGovern MP who sent me helpful prods to keep writing throughout the process. For the member of the Women's PLP who features more than anyone, I must thank Jo Cox's family for being frankly inspirational, and encouraging us all to keep her memory and her legacy alive. I hope I have done her justice.

To my dad and my brothers, their wives and their kids – you are my layers of skin and sometimes that skin gets a really annoying rash that apparently makes for good copy. My dad deserves special thanks for being so bloody-minded as to build me into a stroppy madam. He has been my mom and my dad since my mom died and he does it pretty well, although she was better at Christmas presents. Without my mother- and father-in-law, and their acts of loco parentis, I would have achieved bugger-all and this book would never have got started, let alone finished.

To the men in my life. To my sons, Harry and Danny, for every day making up for the fact that you knackered my pelvic floor. You are the most interesting people I know and I'm sorry that I constantly steal your material when I'm writing. To my husband Tom, the greatest yet most understated feminist I know. You, more than anyone, are on every page of this book. I won't thank you for making our lives so very easy to cope with – I know you would only shrug and say, "It's just how it is bab." You can't take thanks so I'll give you the highest form of Brummy praise and simply say, "you're alright you are."

The real truth of being a successful woman is that I am simply a concoction of the many people in my life. I hope that is reflected here. You have all been ace.